i

Table of Contents

iii

iv

Introduction: I am not writing exclusively about other stupid people

Also: This book is for stupid people. Too bad that you cannot understand it.

It became clear to me early on that I need to provide some instructions for this book. This is not your usual self-help book. I will not be nice to you. I will insult you, and I will insult everything that you like. I will not try to help you very much. This book will not be a shortcut back to the womb for you. It will be brutal.

You are not forced to fix your stupidity, but I will tell you that it is stupid. I am trying to make people aware of what stupidity really is, and of its role in life.

I am not trying to fix your life, but I may be able to explain why you are not enjoying it. Then, you may decide that you do not want to fix your life after all. Or, if you do fix your life, you may thereby break it and become a social pariah that nobody can understand.

This book may help you think, and it may reveal things about life that help you. If not, that is most likely your fault. I am not necessarily trying to change the world, but it would be good if people decided to change for the better.

Before we get too far into the book, I want to say that stupidity has nothing to do with demographic categories such as race, gender, age, or any others. I have a chapter about this later, which you should definitely read if you disagree with me on this. Stupidity also has nothing to do with any medically recognized disability. Stupidity is probably a collection of many unfortunate rehearsed behavioral patterns, but these can and do occur in anyone.

This book is not for or about one person, but I hope that you find part of yourself in it. This book is for and about a bunch of stupid people (humanity) who do stupid things. I wish I could say that you know who you are, but many of you do not.

What then, do I mean by the many times that I refer to a "stupid person?" When I use this phrase, I refer to those who consistently bungle much of their lives, wanting far more than they earn. If you are frustrated much of the time, then you might just be a stupid person. If you think that life would be so much better if only a certain kind of person would disappear or change immediately, then you are probably a certain type of stupid person.

If you have been dissatisfied with your job for long periods of time, or if you become upset after you chat with others online or in person, then you are probably a stupid person. If you are scared or angry for long periods of time but you do not have a serious diagnosed disorder, then you are probably a stupid person. If you think that you cannot possibly be stupid, then you are probably a stupid person. If you have no idea if you are a stupid person or not, then you are probably a stupid person.

In this book, when I tell you that stupid people believe or do something, I mean to say that people approach life suboptimally but comically in this way. Stupid behavior gets near enough to functional behavior to almost make sense, but it fails miserably. The characters portrayed in the Three Stooges are overstated caricatures of stupid people, and it can be fair to say that many stupid people are caricatures of themselves. If I say that stupid people do something that you do, then you may be better off doing something smarter. I am not saying that you are necessarily wrong or contemptible by doing what stupid people do, but I am saying that there are often more fulfilling ways of living. I fully expect that many were confused by what I just said. If so, keep reading, and you may learn a whole new, better way of thinking.

I hope that I offend you at some point as well. If not, then I have not said anything worth saying. Especially in today's world where everyone is offended by everything: a statement is nothing if it does not generate offense. I hope that you also think about it while you are offended, but that may be far too much to ask.

This book can be envisioned as having no admitted audience, because it is for people who are either too stupid or too lazy to have nice things.

Few will admit to such a thing. Instead, many will say that it is "somebody else's fault" that they do not have nice things or do not enjoy them. Others may rationalize self-perceived stupidity to some equally lazy but more comfortable place, where some other stupid people are regarded as at least a little worse, even if one admits to being stupid and dysfunctional.

Many of the people comprising this book's audience have already enshrined laziness and stupidity as their new saviors, and they will not listen to good sense.

This book does not contain statistics, data, or much reference to research. If you are wondering why, then think about it, really. Stupid people hate statistics and data. Nothing makes them run away faster than a research-oriented number, unless that number is made up. Statistics and data can actually discredit an otherwise decent idea, in their minds.

Relying upon statistics and proof could also perpetuate many cultural lies about stupidity that exist in certain circles, especially the lie that statistics and evidence cannot be referenced stupidly. Instead, I will rely on the good old method of saying obvious and/or silly things.

Stupid people also glaze over or repeatedly scream "I'm not crazy!" if you mention a certain word, which I will not mention. It is time to change the name of that discipline, so that some other word can gain exactly the same stigma. I am not necessarily saying this to help stupid people, but I am certainly not going to waste my time by scaring readers away.

Most everyone thinks of most others as being stupid, and they are all generally right. This only matters if you are not where you want to be in life. If you do not enjoy being yourself, then possibly you may need this book more than others do.

It is very stupid to help build a life for yourself that you do not like. It is also stupid to like yourself too much, but society accepts self-love more than self-condemnation. Even certain very loathsome, unattractive, and unskilled stupid people are very much liked in society for one simple reason: they like themselves way too much.

Yes, this book is going to ramble just like this, because it really does not matter that much. It helps to overcome the sadly linear nature of language and text, and you are too stupid to read things that make sense. Your mind is not large enough to retain even short summaries, much less whole books, and therefore this is not a real problem. You are going to focus on irrelevant details instead of opening up your mind to notice the world around you. Stop whining and keep reading.

Stupidity is not necessarily a bad thing. It may even be required to live a successful and fulfilled life. A person's "place" in life may be defined by the stupidities that they accept or are proud of.

The stupidities that you like are selected by yourself, either consciously or subconsciously. Refusing to make a choice in this is simply a choice to maintain a status quo that you had previously chosen in some long-forgotten earlier moment in your life.

You may be wondering why you should bother reading a self-help book that is mainly going to tell you that you are stupid instead of telling you how to fix your life. You should consider that it is stupid to try to fix your life.

The whole concept of "life" is too large for a stupid person to productively grasp. Additionally, "fixing your life" is an extremely ambitious promise that is probably too good to be true. Tackling something like that will stress you out, and you will end up escaping from that and escaping from yourself and your own stupid self-demands, in one way or another.

You are better off not listening to those who say that they will fix your life, because anyone who says this is a con artist who will charge too much for the little or nothing that they will do. Just wait for the point where they ask you for fifty bucks to fix your life a little more than they did earlier. The smart ones, mythical creatures that they are, know that it is essentially addictive to feel like you are fixing your life because of what someone else told you.

Lazy people are thrilled by the idea that their life is fixing itself through little of their own effort. Fixing your life is what you can do, not what someone else does. Others can be helpful in pointing out things that you had not considered, but it is your responsibility to follow up on it.

If you still want to fix your life, even though I told you all of the above, then focus on things that you can understand. Life-fixing could result as a side-effect of fixing more easily understood problems that you are much better off addressing, instead of wasting time trying to grasp some highly abstract concept such as life. Chances are that even if you did fully understand life, this knowledge would only make your life worse because nobody would be able to understand you.

This book may help you figure out how to improve things of actual value in your life, but only if you want that. Many other readers will not change and may not need to change.

If you want to understand stupidity and consider its role in shaping people and societies, then keep reading. Self-help could result as an unintended side-effect from reading this book.

I do not guarantee that this book will help you. This is not because I lack the confidence of a con artist, but because I do not wish to employ dishonesty and hyperbole as a tool to convince you of things.

Stupid people essentially beg and plead for con artistry to save them from the effort of thinking, and therefore they will not listen to plain sense, but that is your problem and not mine. Please realize that I am not trying to convince you of anything. Believing accurate things is your responsibility, and only extremely stupid people rely on others to tell them what to think.

Stupidity can be said to have a central tenet, although stupid people need to remain consciously unaware of it, lest they break it too. The tenet of stupidity is that an idea can only be good if it works even when carried out wrongly and badly.

This tenet leads stupid people to live a lifelong mission of breaking good ideas that do not satisfy its excessive demands. Stupid people then turn to bad ideas instead, especially those that are so impossible as to be untestable.

If a stupid idea can be used to annoy a smart person, it will become exalted and sanctified in stupid culture. Such annoying ideas are at least momentarily adopted as undeniably true by stupid people, even if this soon results in self-destruction.

Despite all the above, stupidity does not always lead to disastrous results. A subtle example of this is in the apparent necessity of change under different scenarios.

When things are relatively good, we are much more resistant to adopting slightly better alternatives. When things are terrible, we are more willing to adopt multiple simultaneous radical changes that can lead to a better overall scenario.

This may be why, for instance, some of history's most technologically backwards cultures (I am looking at you, western medicine) achieved groundbreaking discoveries only after much-needed major changes were made to catch up with the rest of the world.

The result can be a combination of newly adopted good practices with a few retained good, and possibly only tangentially related, practices. A better than expected result can be achieved when a society reforms in this way.

In other words, while many know that the perfect is the enemy of that which is merely good, the good is also the enemy of that which is slightly better.

It usually does not work like this however, in part because stupid people would much rather imitate badly than innovate well. Additionally, stupid people habitually go overboard and bungle things: either changing too much or making bad conditions persist for too long. I will address the thought processes behind such mistakes as the book goes on.

I could go on for a while discussing why stupidity is important, but this is mostly well-understood. One thing that you may not have considered is this: stupid people control the world in a very real way.

Everything that you do must be simplified so that other stupid people can understand it. Nice things must be left by the wayside so that stupid people can have their way. Good decisions must be dropped because they were too much for stupid people to understand. In these ways, stupid people can have a buffering effect on society. This is not always bad, but it frequently feels bad.

Finally, please realize that I am not talking about mentally ill people. That is a whole other topic to itself. I will spend some time later talking about people who consider themselves mentally ill when they are not. Regardless of whether you have a mental illness, please remember that it is possible to have a health issue and be stupid at the same time. What I have to say about that is: always try to improve your life. Always strive to make things better. Do not accept any assumed reality of weakness or inferiority simply because you are aware of a problem that you have. Many other people are strong while not being aware of their problems, after all. Mere awareness of a problem should not make it impossible to handle.

Chapter 1: You are so stupid that you do not even know what words mean

I would rather start this book off differently, but you have little hope of understanding it, because you do not know what many simple words mean. You should not try to change that, because you would most likely hurt yourself trying to be more intelligent than you are. That would be probably worse than whatever it was that you were previously doing, and so you should not try it.

Still, if you are going to try to read this, you will be told some things that you should know for your own good. Then you may transition into being an informed stupid person, which is different from, but not necessarily better than, an ignorant stupid person.

Stupid people do not know what you are saying. They may not be listening, but even if listening they would still get it wrong.

Concentration is in very short supply where stupid people are concerned. Frequently, they will assume that you said the opposite of what you really said, because they cannot hear you over the endless repetition of the same old thoughts inside their heads. Some of these thoughts may circulate inside their heads for decades, not changing at all.

These thoughts are like a spinning wheel that distracts them for most of their lives. Anything that breaks them out of this can make them feel like thousand tons has been lifted from their shoulders. Without this, there is little hope of getting a stupid person to actually understand what you are saying unless you are repeating these same circulating thoughts back to them.

Communication functions mainly on a primal level with stupid people, where they focus on the sound of your voice as an indicator of mood, and upon emphasis as an indicator of meaning. The actual word often does not matter much, except when it functions as a keyword that triggers a rehearsed response.

All of this generally proceeds in broken and dysfunctional ways, except when multiple people arrive together at the same set of mistaken conclusions to be on the same wavelength. This is also a primal process, involving recognized social roles stemming especially from dominance.

I had a friend who became annoyed when I said that she was assertive. Assertiveness is a good thing, in case you were not aware, but she was not aware. She was both stupid and maybe a bit more than simply assertive, and therefore she was not afraid to demonstrate those qualities together by complaining and being offended. She also was in the habit of never questioning her often incorrect assumptions. This did not help her at all in this circumstance, although it is a great life strategy in proper doses. It did help me realize that people are stupid, and that even "intelligent" university graduates are incredibly stupid people who do not understand simple words. I am not excluding myself from this. I suspect that you thought I was. This is because you are stupid.

Even if you did not think that I was excluding myself from being stupid, do not congratulate yourself. Chances are that this was due to simple luck, and that you will soon do something else that is very stupid. After all, nobody can be intelligent all the time, and nobody can be stupid all the time (despite the best efforts of some). As they say, even a broken clock is right twice a day.

Oh, in case you still do not know what "assertive" means, get off your lazy ass and look it up. Google is your long-neglected friend. Some people in the past would have killed to have Google to save them the effort of getting out of their chairs to grab a dictionary. They were stupid too.

Somebody may claim that some people are more stupid, or more frequently stupid, than others. This is usually said to incorrectly justify oneself or to justify some very stupid actions. If you focus on the stupidity of others far more than your own, you are building a world of frustration for yourself.

Rest assured that you are stupid, and that you almost certainly have no idea how stupid you or others are. Anything said to the contrary falls under the category of "stupid people manipulating stupid people."

By the way, I will not bother much in qualifying further comments with superfluous statements such as "almost certainly" in the rest of this book, because you would not need such intellectual crutches if you were not so stupid.

It is possible, but exceedingly unlikely, that a rare non-stupid person will be reading this, and my inclusion of "almost certainly" in a sentence would cover such a near-impossibility, making the sentence crystal clear to this unicorn-like mythical reader. The existence of such a reader is extremely unlikely because nature abhors intelligence, and it is much more likely that any intelligent person will be murdered with rocks, poison, gunfire, knives, or something else before reading this. Regardless, it is not worth our time for me to type that and for you to read qualifiers such as "almost certainly," because they are obvious. If you cannot understand simple realities, it is not my fault for not handing out crutches to you. Stop being lazy and try to think, or not if it hurts too much.

Yes, I do provide crutches elsewhere, because I took pity on you (I should not), but nobody can accurately anticipate all the intellectual crutches needed by a lazy person. If I gave you all the crutches in the world, you would invent a new affliction. It is therefore much better for you to not need so many crutches. Or at least, if you must use a crutch, please try to be aware of it and do not assume that it is a necessary part of communication.

It is an accident of human thought that language is designed to reflect the wrong beliefs of stupid people who believed in all sorts of impossible absolutes. How about fixing the language, so that it becomes easier to say accurate things than it is to apparently make sweeping generalizations that are obviously inaccurate? No? Then shut up and stop your pitiful whining. It is much easier to speak with conviction by making wild generalizations, than it is to apparently waffle about by being very accurate with wishy-washy qualifiers.

Some previous book pointed out that stupidity can only occur in an individual that has capacity for intelligence, because stupidity indicates an unfulfilled expectation of intelligence. Trees and rocks are not stupid, for instance, but people are. I cannot remember who wrote that, because I am stupid too.

In case the previous words did not make it obvious: when a person for some reason is not able to figure out something that they should be able to figure out, that "some reason" is stupidity.

You may be wondering, or at least have some stupid opinion, about why I need to repeat the word "stupid" so much. I do this because you would forget if not constantly reminded.

Every worthwhile idea in existence only became noticed by stupid people after it was repeated countless times, even by those who did not understand it. It would not be remembered if not repeated so much. Many bad ideas get repeated countless times too, but that is because you are still trying to decide if they are good or bad. I took a few instances of the word "stupid" out during editing. Try to be thankful.

And yes, I am highly confident that you, the reader, are stupid. The more fervently that you may disagree with this or try to escape its applicability, the more likely it is that you really are simply stupid and lazy on top of it. I will explain this later, because your head can only hold so much.

Another stupid friend illustrated one day that he did not understand what I meant by "common." I tried to point out that some stupid quality was common one day, and he assumed that I intended to say that royalty did not do such things. This could not be further from the truth. First, by "common" I had meant "frequent." Second, kings, queens, dukes, etc. are stupid too. I later learned that he was excessively proud of his claim to some very minor hereditary title, indicating that he was royally stupid.

The point of this chapter, because I suspect that you forgot, is that you have little hope of understanding what I am trying to say because you do not know what words mean. You are not going to learn, and so this chapter is wholly written in vain. I bet you do not know what I mean by "vain." I bet you think this chapter is about you. It is.

Some words are completely misunderstood because people think that connotations are denotations. It never occurs to these people that they could be wrong of course, because they are astoundingly stupid.

Dictionaries have adapted to this by including some previously incorrect meanings and spellings, so that we can feel better about being wrong. This may be a good idea, because we are not getting any smarter anytime soon.

Connotations often stem from stupid emotions wrongly attached to a word, very frequently attached while watching television shows, movies, and plays seen during formative years. This happens in part because people do not know what these words mean, and they try to gain the meaning from the context.

In the case of spoken entertainment, the context includes the way that an actor delivers a word. A word used sarcastically can thereby gain a generally accepted connotation that is opposite from its denotation. The way that an actor uses and says a word is very influential if the actor is skilled, and words can be ruined for decades or centuries simply because of the way that it was used in one popular form of entertainment. Such connotations have far more force than denotations ever will.

At this stage, clever stupid people out there may point out that the multiple actual versus perceived meanings of words are a massive stumbling block for people who want to appreciate written and spoken art forms. I certainly agree with these stupid people, but I must point out that language is in some ways an intelligence test.

More complex languages can perform more complex tests, but even simple languages expand in complexity to what a society desires. People who are smart enough will get it, but as I have said, smart people are like unicorns. Those who do not understand will greatly outnumber those who do, unless you are skilled enough to communicate on their stupid level where words do not exactly mean what the dictionary says.

Effectively-used words are therefore almost always at least slightly deceptive, because people must exaggerate or otherwise depart from denotation to communicate in an impactful way. This deception may be very welcome, because it could communicate that you like someone sincerely. By this deception, you indicate that you are willing to use enough effort to artfully deceive.

A lazy lie will not do, instead communicating that you do not really find the matter to be worth your attention. Therefore, in this bizarre world that we have created for ourselves, sincerity is communicated by indicating that we care enough to put some real effort into deception.

We can hardly say such words as "try" without someone telling us, "Don't try, do it!" Never mind that you cannot do anything without trying to do it. This highlights the sharp distinction between what words actually mean versus what people think when they hear them. This is caused by stupidity from more than one source, not simply from the stupid person who is telling you to proceed impossibly. The other stupid people contributing to this are the lazy ones who focus too much on otherwise innocent words such as "try" when predicting their own failures unreasonably. Since none of us can spare the effort to say something with insight, the response is, "Don't try, do it!" rather than, "Are you so sure that you will fail? Try harder and you can succeed."

You may gain from this the concept that people discover your personality from the ways and degree in which you sincerely depart from the truth. This will be discussed at great length later.

Some people who work hard to manipulate others, will consistently redefine words to their own benefit. Good and bad people disagree over the definitions of good and bad, for instance.

Differences between denotation and connotation often stem from the clever brand of stupidity, but many do not.

For instance, there are very few ways that using "articulate" to praise someone can sound good, and many in which it sounds bad. Never mind that it is definitely good to be articulate. Much praise is insincere, and praise for being "articulate," told to your face, probably is insincere and probably comes from someone who expected incoherent and bumbling grunts from you instead. It reveals that even in this simple, shallow culture, flatterers are still disliked. It also reveals that we are all keenly focused on determining whether people really like us or not, and that we do not expect them to speak simple truth about it.

Few things are worse for an interpersonal relationship than trying to say that you like someone, only to be revealed as a clumsy and insincere flatterer instead. We like our flattery to sound sincere, even when it is not.

Rarely-used words have connotations that are far more frequent than their denotations, and some are only understood within a certain phrase. They are crutches when used in these ways, but they also cause considerable confusion when someone with a real vocabulary is speaking or writing. Frugal is a word like that.

Many will say that they do not want to be frugal, because they think it means "like an old person" in a bad way. It means "thrifty," and there are plenty of young frugal people, but they believe that they are thrifty or not wasteful. They may go on for hours explaining the virtues of how some role model culture or person was not wasteful. However, they do not believe that the word frugal describes them, and they would not use such a word for anything that they like. You cannot call them frugal without making them at least a little annoyed because they feel misunderstood. After all, they are simply thrifty, not old! This is one of the reasons why slang is constantly being invented. Older words may be entirely misunderstood, but a new and effective slang word, which may have meant either nothing or something different the previous year, would be well-understood.

Words that once were effective warnings can become words of praise, because we are very stupid and backwards. It is no longer a warning or insult to call someone "reckless," because we know that reckless people are exciting rulebreakers who benefit from the risks that they take. The cultural narrative states that you can benefit from surviving these risks alongside them, because everyone who is disturbed or hurt by their risks is simply weak. Generations of exciting stories have taught you this, and you remember this because you are stupid and have a much greater capacity for learning nonsense than sense.

Who is more exciting, after all: the rule-breaker or the one who follows every rule? Because of all this, you think that "reckless" is high praise for someone. Calling someone reckless can help them secure very valuable things in life, because people are profoundly stupid.

A special case of not understanding words is that stupid people have no idea what optimism, pessimism, and realism are. Stupid people think that either optimism or pessimism is realism, depending on what they prefer at a given time. Instead, reality is not biased one way or the other.

Some lazy stupid people perpetuate this error by insisting that reality or a person can only be entirely optimistic or pessimistic. This type of laziness is mainly found in the enterprise of thinking about thinking, because the more abstract nature of all this will serve to hide glaring errors. It is difficult to find another situation where laziness can be so stealthy, but imagine an automotive mechanic who always uses duct tape to replace parts, instead of doing it properly. Someone who does not care about automotives would not immediately catch them, but very soon anyone who actually uses their vehicle will discover the issue when the vehicle breaks again. Laziness produces vehicles of thought that are similarly dysfunctional.

Laziness in perception, conceptualization, or communication is uninspiring for yourself and others, producing thoughts that may seem fine to other lazy people, up until the moment that such thoughts need to be used.

Let us go on a rant for a moment. A great many stupid people believe that "I have accepted this as possible" can only mean, "I want this to happen." They cannot understand how anyone could notice and accept a possibility that was not previously desired. This suggests that denial has been chosen as the one and only savior of stupid minds. It indicates that functional adult behavior is not even comprehensible at all by such unfortunate individuals.

Mature adults, ones who functionally handle real responsibilities and do serious things, must be open-minded to the possibility that something good or bad could happen. They do not only notice and accept possibilities that fit their preferred emotional mindset. This is because mature people are equipped to handle both prosperity and adversity, as long as they are properly aware of their surroundings. People who do important things cannot afford to twist optimism or pessimism into accepting the possibility of only good or bad news. Stupid people are instead only capable of existing at one extreme or the other: only accepting that something good could happen, or never accepting that something good could happen.

Getting back to the prior point, both optimism and pessimism are inherently inaccurate, and neither will ever be realistic. Yet, both have their uses as concepts. Blanket optimism is an option that helps you feel better about everything in general, but gets you scammed more often than blanket pessimism does. Pessimism will never solve a problem for you, but it does give you plenty of excuses.

It is much better to employ optimism and pessimism situationally to what they are best-suited to help predict, instead of lazily using one or the other for everything. Being optimistic about your own skills, but pessimistic about the veracity of e-mail offers, for instance, is the way to go. I do not expect you to do this, because I am pessimistic about your willingness to exit the metaphorical womb and give up using laziness and stupidity to evade responsibility for your problems.

It would be a pleasant surprise if you did stop being so lazy and stupid. So do it, just to prove me wrong. It is only because of properly used optimism that I am bothering to make you aware of these issues and telling you that there is an amazingly effective alternative to being lazy and stupid. That alternative is called living with enthusiasm.

The very frequent inability of stupid people to distinguish "some" from either "all" or "none" is the cause of much misunderstanding of words. "Some" can never be just "some" to a stupid person. Depending on mood and personality, it will be assigned to one extreme or another. This renders "some" into merely a mild euphemism to stupid people, referring to extremes instead of something existing somewhere between extremes. Never mind that reality consists almost entirely of gradual variation, with very few absolutes. Stupid people have no use for your wimpy "sometimes" or "usually," even when "always" and "never" are far less accurate.

"Why is this?" you may be stupidly wondering to yourself. This is because stupid people are shaped mainly by bizarre interactions with other stupid people. It is not different from the "try" example above.

In past interactions between younger stupid people, accurate words may have been used by weak individuals who focused too much on the complexity of the world and upon its limitations, getting one thing or another wrong but using highly accurate words to arrive to these wrong conclusions. All this becomes tiresome in many ways, and especially so when it derails fun. The stupid solution to this situation is to choose the opposite, avoiding accurate words even when they are useful.

Stupid people communicate and think like children, or to put it differently, they do not increase their communication or thinking skills beyond what they had in their formative years.

I should mention here that there is a certain kind of stupid person who insists that others follow some rules on grammar, word usage, spelling, punctuation, and so forth, or they cannot tolerate you. This type of stupid person probably will not change, and nobody should tolerate them. They otherwise do not differ from other types of excessively narrow-minded stupid people, and they have the greatest resemblance to the type of stupid person who "knows only one truth." They can only be happy while living according to explicit rules and enforcing them, never being able to deal with anything outside those narrow rules. These types of stupid people are annoying, even when the one thing they know is true. There are plenty of other people who are not tolerated in this world, and it should not be much trouble to add these to the list.

I suppose you thought at one time in this book that I will call you an idiot, imbecile, or moron. I have said such things in the past. This is because I am fully aware that you have little or no idea what these words mean. Since these words are so strongly misunderstood, they are very effective for communicating things that they do not mean. They are much more effective, if you want to get a point across, than a correctly-used word.

Some people think it is great praise to be called "stupid" for instance. Only "stupid" people can have horse sense, according to their narrative. Their decades of stupidity have supposedly taught them things that smart people supposedly cannot know. Some of those same people would take offense to being called a "moron."

Some of you stupid people somehow know that idiot, imbecile, and moron have been used for centuries, but that they are also outdated diagnostic terms. They were used by stupid researchers to vaguely compare a small number of adults to average children of a certain age. This was based primarily on the mistaken assumption that adults are normally smart. Instead, adults are merely well-practiced post-puberty babies who have grown more experienced at crying.

How many two-year-olds could read this book, by the way? I am not aware of any. Therefore, you are not an idiot. You probably had some vague idea of that already, but you would still likely be insulted for some stupid reason if I called you an idiot.

Would you be insulted if I called you a Toyota car or the planet Neptune? Probably not. Instead, you would probably dismiss such an obviously out-of-place and ineffective comment. That would be the proper response to being called an "idiot" as well, but stupid people do not respond appropriately. An insult not heard is not effective, just like a misunderstood or misapplied insult misses the mark. Stupid people feel insulted much of the time, when smart people would not feel insulted at all.

As discussed earlier, we live in a world where connotation delivers the real point of a word. This can rob us of the emotional comfort that could be gained from ignoring inappropriately-used insults.

Stupid people are somehow open to the idea that they could be correctly called an idiot, being deeply troubled because they believe that somebody may be telling them an unpleasant truth. "What if I really am an idiot?" and, "What if everybody else is smarter than me?" you may be thinking stupidly to yourself on some level. Do not worry: someone calling you an idiot is not telling the truth, but you are frightfully stupid, just like nearly everyone else. Congratulations on fitting in.

This whole fascinating pattern of backwardness and irrationality in may derive from our long history of using vague noises to communicate. These noises likely developed a deeply ingrained meaning that makes far more sense to us than a sequence of letters or correctly chosen syllables. Therefore, verbal communication is not crucially dependent on word choice alone.

Choosing a word that is inappropriate, yet using a strong or stimulating tone of voice, may even have a greater intended effect than using the same tone of voice with a correct word. Probably this is because anybody can easily be correct, but it takes a creative person to make a wrong word sound right. This is because you and others are stupid.

Many stupid people spend most of their days yelling nonsense at their children or pets under the guise of disciplining them. I say that this is nonsense, even though the words themselves may be occasionally useful. Any useful words are hidden under heaps of nonsense or are hidden by the same disdainful tone of voice every time, and therefore nobody listens, and good behavior does not result. Instead, the children and pets more or less perceive that you are being threatening in some way that is often not connected to whatever they did wrong. The real communication in this world stems from the sounds, expressions, and other factors that are not in the dictionary. Idiotic, yes? Not really.

Chapter 2: The question of the existence of smart people

You may be ready to point out, hopefully much earlier than now, that there is the word "smart" that ought to have some purpose, and that there may be some smart people in this world.

I do not absolutely deny the existence of smart people, but I suggest that they are so rare that I can mostly ignore them while writing this book. Also, nobody understands smart person, and so it is very likely that they would be destroyed in some way before they encountered this book. Finally, smart people have less need of this book than stupid people do, and are therefore not the intended audience.

All that said, if you are reading this but think you are smart, then you should continue reading. Such a horribly mistaken belief indicates that you are the worst kind of stupid person.

I know that I have already defined stupidity, but let us keep going. I have used the word "lazy" a few times now, and stupid people may lapse into thinking that stupidity is simply laziness.

One could say that stupidity is mental laziness, but one would be at least a little inaccurate. Instead, stupidity can be called more accurately a lack of mental discipline. Here again I run the risk of using misunderstood words. Stupid people hate discipline, because they consider discipline to mean nothing more than a tragic avoidance of fun.

Just try it: exercise a little discipline and you will be the target of the "all work and no play" lecture. Nobody ever gets tired of repeating that lecture. Here again the all-or-nothing mentality of stupid people appears.

Stupid people cannot imagine that you could be exercising the right amount of discipline. They can only believe in too much or too little, because they cannot imagine that life is made up of real continuous variations between abstract endpoints. Stupid people instead live in a world of rigid opposites with supposedly obvious moral differences labeling these opposites, never perceiving that these extremes are conceptual crutches and that reality ignores such silly things.

Let us dwell on some related ideas for a bit. Stupid people believe that smart people are simply a different type of stupid person who is merely odd. They think that smart people have all the frequent failings of stupid people, but with an eccentric and difficult-to-understand slant to it. This is why it is often necessary to "dumb it down to their level" in order to effectively communicate with stupid people. This is comparable to some process where a three-dimensional object would need to be cut down to two-dimensions.

There are many reasons why it is difficult for stupid people to understand smart people, but the lack of adherence to the tropes of stupidity is one of the main reasons. It would be an enlightening, mind-blowing experience for a stupid person to ever understand a smart person. Discipline could be required, and goodness knows that discipline means no fun ever again in the mind of a stupid person.

The tropes of stupidity are shortcuts to help even stupid people understand each other. This is because people are understood through their failings, habitual mistakes, and shortcomings, more than by what they do right. You will occasionally be partially understood through positive qualities, but those qualities are expected and therefore are to some degree uninteresting and not fully instructive. Bad qualities are deeply understood, and they make up the chief part of what people understand about you. A person without good qualities would be understood very well, and would be liked by some, but a person without bad qualities would be universally misunderstood, and would be disliked or ignored.

But what is a smart person really? Smart people are good at many things that may not appear related at first glance. If you are bad at many things, but very good at only a few things, then you are probably stupid. There could be many possible causes of this. You may not want to practice or learn. You may be filling your head with useless thoughts that serve only as busy-work for your mind. You may believe that it is bad to be intelligent. You may be so chemically dependent or have such bad behavioral practices that your mind is hobbled. There are many possible causes, and they could be occurring simultaneously.

A considerable amount of cultural thought has historically been devoted to human dignity. Stupid people are the counterargument to this. They remind us that people retain the ability to fail, no matter how much is achieved by smart people.

Stupid people are characterized by cognitive and emotional weaknesses, and they are somewhat aware of this. They will either become proud of their failings, or they will become morbidly despondent because of them, but they refuse to perceive anything with any sort of balanced or accurate perspective.

Stupid people respond to human potential by meticulously and thoroughly squandering it. They make it seem like humans can only achieve destruction or pointlessness, and they can make us wonder how anything has ever been achieved in human existence.

When a few smart people succeed and prove to be inspirations to many, stupid people work even harder to make all achievements seem to be impossible for humans, maybe requiring space aliens to swoop down and tell us which is the pointy end of a stick. Stupid people will make all past achievements appear to be clever deceptions that actually serve to reinforce the negative aspects of human existence.

But oh, you smart people, if you exist, beware: if stupid people do not understand what kind of failings you have, they will make something up. They may latch onto small flaws or momentary lapses and exaggerate them, or they may fabricate something that is entirely without any basis. They will never abandon this misunderstanding of you, regardless of contrary evidence, because their world would be shattered without converting everyone into components that make sense in their own twisted world view.

Because stupid people are so numerous, it is a good idea to invent a flaw for yourself that you find acceptable. After selecting this, act the part. This will guide stupid people into assigning a trait to you that you find acceptable in comparison to some much worse alternatives. It helps tremendously if this flaw makes them want to be you.

The old concept of the Seven Deadly Sins is a good guide for this. Which of them would you like to have, or which do you find least objectionable? Society generally prefers Lust or some revised version of Gluttony, and so it is a good idea to pretend to have one of those, but I leave the decision up to you.

Just remember when you do this: deception works best when you are also convinced of it. When you can convincingly fabricate sincerity, enough to even fool yourself, the world will love you.

Chapter 3: How to deal with stupid people

Yes, this is a book for stupid people, and I am telling them how to deal with stupid people. This should come as no surprise, because there is hardly any other type of person out there.

But let us get to the point. In order to better deal with stupid people in your life, it helps to first learn how to deal with yourself. I know this is an unsatisfying answer for lazy people, but the one stupid person that you cannot get rid of is yourself. You are also the only person that you can reliably change.

You can change yourself, but you cannot change what others think. After you improve yourself, you may need to constantly struggle with people who think that you still have the previous kind of stupid. They will not believe that you have a whole new kind of stupid unless it is something cataclysmic enough to get their attention.

The types of things that gain the attention of stupid people are things that they enthusiastically agree with or things that they can use against you. They use both of these on an instinctive level, and so there is no point in trying to reason with this process. Instead, be aware of it and plan for it.

There are many reasons why stupid people are annoying, and in each case our annoyance is due to incorrect beliefs that we have. Stupid people stubbornly and proudly adhere to incorrect beliefs.

Our expectation is that people should adopt increasingly accurate beliefs whenever they think about something. Yet, how do we know that our beliefs are more accurate? In most cases, there is at least some perceivable inaccuracy in our own beliefs.

Stupid people would much rather pay attention to the small inaccuracies in your beliefs than to reconsider the vast inaccuracies in their own. Chances are that you have not verified your answer any more than they have, but let us assume for argument's sake that you did. Even then, it is extremely rare that anybody believes anything that is tolerably accurate about a controversial issue. Instead, nearly everyone believes something that is entertaining but hardly true.

Why should we expect the world to turn upside-down to such an extreme degree that stupid people will believe accurate things? This is like expecting Great White Sharks to change their minds and become vegetarians. Or did you think that you were dealing with the mythical beast known as a "smart person?" Why would you believe that after getting this far in this book?

Get rid of those incorrect assumptions and expectations, and stop denying reality. You are not dealing with smart people. Expect them to be wrong. Expect them to be tenaciously wrong. Expect them to enjoy their wrongness so much that they will believe that they are infinitely smarter than you because you refuse to adopt their stupid position. Expect them to try to mock and troll you because you believe that accurate conclusions are better than inaccurate ones. Expect them to enjoy their power in almost alchemically converting ludicrous falsehoods into truths. Expect them to refuse to adopt good sense, because good sense is a mysterious and frightening thing to stupid people.

Nothing is more futile than trying to get stupid people to believe anything that makes sense. How much time do you plan to waste before accepting this? You can consider going back to those stupid expectations after you see Great White Sharks naturally going after broccoli instead of blood.

This is not to say that unilateral rejection of falsehood and inaccuracy is any better than what stupid people do. Have you ever met a person who can only think literally and only in a very restricted scope, never making creative or unique connections, never truly getting any type of joke or metaphor? Such a computer-like stupid person is what you get when the wacky web of lies disappears from a person's mind.

These benign lies aid in thinking laterally because they assist in making connections that a literal-minded individual would not make. A person who can only accept obviously and immediately relevant truths at any given moment, is a dull person indeed. That is why we exercise our minds with juggled inaccuracies constantly. We do this part as exercises that increase intelligence, and in part as exercises that increase social skills.

Even very simple minds can accept truths, but it takes a person who is both skillful and creative to wade through a jungle of inaccuracies while dealing with all of them in fun ways but remaining in touch with the truth. Societal networks of lies are therefore tests of a person's mental and emotional fitness.

There are shortcuts through the wacky web of lies. This is in part why the choice of words in communication does not always matter to stupid people. Instead, the attitude used in communication means far more.

A well-chosen attitude employed with inaccurate words will be far more successful in communication than accurate words used without an effective attitude. I refer to an effective attitude in communication as speaking with conviction.

Very frequently, an energetically communicated but incorrect point will become more accepted than a correct but lazily or ineffectively communicated point. So do not be lazy. Right. I expected the keening whines that I heard in response to that. Telling someone to not be lazy is like telling them to not be stupid, but the laziness of otherwise intelligent individuals can have extreme consequences.

"But what should I do instead of trying to make stupid people believe right things?" I hear some of you whine. Listen to them and understand the stupidity of their opinions. What else are you going to do?

Frustration will not help here. If you thoroughly understand their positions, then you have a better chance of gaining better insight or explaining their incorrectness to someone else. Stupid people refuse to consider others' beliefs if they do not agree with the attitudes and perceived biases of said stupid people (because why consider anything that is inherently and infinitely wrong?).

Even knowing that someone is stupid does not always help, because some stupid people are talented in finding unexpected stupid things to say or believe. Despite all this, frustration over disagreement comes entirely from our own minds, in part because we expect impossible things, but also because of cognitive dissonance within ourselves.

Those two big, scary words, cognitive dissonance, hide a concept that everyone understands on some level. We generally know that inner doubt indicates a weakness of some sort. I say "generally" here even though I promised to not do things like that, because stupid people can always find a way to foul something up and interpret it wrongly. Cognitive dissonance can take the form of several different emotions: defensiveness, frustration, anger, and emotional exhaustion, for instance.

Stupid people frequently believe that anger is strength, but only when they want to agree with the anger. When they want to disagree, they recognize that it is weakness instead. In both circumstances, they understand and perceive the cognitive dissonance in a primal way. Most everyone knows that you are experiencing cognitive dissonance, even if they do not understand it in a rational way.

It is regrettable that simpler words for cognitive dissonance are not better known. A greatly disproportionate amount of focus is placed upon lesser concepts such as "confidence," when confidence itself is a lack of cognitive dissonance concerning one's own abilities.

The cause of the cognitive dissonance is (partly) this: even if you say that you can only accept your own idea, you know on some level that agreement emerges from discussion and analysis, not from insisting upon agreement without meaningful discussion.

You can expect people to agree with the better idea, but on some level you know that you are also communicating something that is at least partially wrong. These are all realities of human communication. Make everyone happier by shutting up and listening unless the opportunity arises to properly explain your point. This opportunity may not arise, and that is not a problem.

Convincing a stupid person is not done with reason after all, but through superior attitude. Any visible or voiced frustration, anger, desperation, or outrage on your part only indicates your own doubts or denial of reality.

Or, just use the anger to vent off frustration and give up on the idea of using words for communication. That is a valid choice, even if it does not directly communicate much.

Many will tell you that wisdom includes understanding what you do not know. Fewer will tell you of the benefits of understanding what other people do not know.

Nearly every part of life is impacted by the slight thrill generated when cognitive dissonance is triggered. Cursing is cathartic because people feel on some level that they should not be cursing. If they were encouraged by everyone to curse, they would stop. This is not as good as it may sound, because then we would all have to turn to some other outlet to get rid of stress, probably more harmful than simply saying some harmless but naughty word. Plus, if nobody was cursing, how else would you know who is naughty out there? Such matters are very important.

Stupid people refuse to do things in a productive way, instead willfully choosing regress or stagnation instead of progress. Stupid people do not usually say that they want to go backwards. Many want something that they call progress, except that their vision of progress is incredibly stupid.

As discussed previously, challenging our own wrong beliefs is the way to deal with this. Consider that stupid people are well-practiced in making bad decisions, and hardly or not at all practiced in making good ones. Additionally, your idea of progress is probably deeply flawed as well.

Trying to actually understand alternative visions is a very useful thing, because it helps you to understand your own position. You cannot say that you fully understand something until you can explain exactly why alternatives are rejected.

Sometimes you may have to wade through massive amounts of crud to get to the actual ideas behind a stupid person's position, because stupid people overcomplicate things. Some stupid people even make conscious efforts to hide their bad ideas under annoying piles of useless ones, piles so large that nobody could ever read them all, because they know that their ideas cannot stand up to any scrutiny.

In situations where bad ideas are heaped under annoying or misleading ideas, consider ignoring excessive crud or scrapping the entire system and starting over. Yes, I know that stupid people will be against that. Maybe write a book about stupid people instead. I have heard that this has been tried before.

Another reason that stupid people are annoying is that they tend to gain apparently undeserved success and influence. Here again, frustration is due to our own incorrect beliefs.

Why, for instance, should stupid people make appropriate decisions when hiring or promoting anyone? It is shocking that anything works in a world full of stupid people, and we are lucky that we have what we have. I would tell you to look at the hidden skills that stupid people have, but this requires mental gymnastics. You may be able to notice the great cleverness that stupid people employ in the pursuit of laziness, trolling, or otherwise bad things. A great many stupid people do these bad things because they are too paralyzed by fear of failure to intentionally attempt anything constructive. Such is our stupid society.

Chapter 4: The power and pitfalls of irrationality

Irrationality is a very valuable thing, and it has helped the human race advance. This is because it is not possible to know and understand everything about the world around you. Some things will be unknown or misunderstood, and irrationality helps us consider and deal with things that do not add up. This is why you do not lock up in the same way that a computer would, when you are confronted by errors and other things that do not make sense.

A special form of self-delusion allows you to simultaneously deal with alternative possibilities. Because at least one of the alternatives is likely not present in the real world, the self-delusion called "imagination" must be used to give it proper consideration. Some stupid people fail miserably at this, but I suspect that at least some of them are faking it.

Make no mistake (or go ahead and make one if that is all you can do): irrationality is not always a good thing, and it will not solve all of your problems. Even when irrationality helps you through a problem, it does so because it is simply good enough for this purpose, not because it yields accurate answers.

Stupid and lazy people frequently misuse irrationality on things that are easily understood, causing problems when the results are predictably irrational as well.

Irrationality on some level can help you deal with bizarre things that happen in your life, but it will usually not help you solve a mathematics problem. It will also not help you deal properly with people who expect rational behavior. Humans may have been called, stupidly, a "rational animal," but we are also the only animal that has such a strong capacity for irrationality.

Best belonging here is another point: stupid people are not unskilled at thinking, and they are not always slow. Instead, stupid people often do a great deal of thinking, but in inefficient and/or self-destructive ways.

Stupid people create incredibly complex, but also useless or harmful, systems of thought: Fortresses of Stupidity. These fortresses can also be like Rat Tunnels of thought. They are complex, confusing, and are more informative about the thinker than about anything else. They can house things that have been necessary to the thinker, and indeed they are not always bad.

Well-designed fortresses and rat tunnels serve a good purpose, but a stupid person can be compared to a rat who makes an overly complex set of tunnels that serve to get it lost, drowned, or eaten by predators, instead of serving as a good home for the rat.

The problem with stupid people is therefore not a lack of complexity in thought. The problem is instead the misused, and often excessive, complexity that can needlessly tire them out or misdirect them into making bizarre and elaborate Fortresses of Stupidity that protect pitifully inaccurate thoughts.

Maybe weak thoughts need a great deal of protection, but they are not worth it. It is much better to go to the "trouble" of finding a useful thought that accurately fits reality. Such a strong thought does not need protection, and the amount of trouble taken to arrive at it will be less than what is required to make a pointless fortress. Stupid people, after wasting all their time and energy protecting and endlessly reliving stupid thoughts, become too tired to consider thoughts that are worth having.

But why? You may be asking this, and rightly so. Consider life-threatening situations. It is often, but not always, useful to have accurate beliefs about these situations. It is also often useful to have inaccurate beliefs that are good enough for the moment. It is usually not useful to be paralyzed in doubt. Being more or less wrong, but not in doubt, is therefore favored over being too doubt-stricken to act. It would certainly be even better to always arrive at the right answer, but that is only possible in stories.

During my education, I encountered readings stating that our senses are fallible. I thought this sounded silly, because I could see and hear things just fine. There was a chair, the teacher, the clock on the wall, nothing wrong. As I grew older, I realized that in a way senses are very fallible.

Our interpretation of sensory feedback is often completely off kilter even if our eyes and ears do their jobs. We may see and hear things accurately with our eyes and ears, but our brains filter information and do not process it perfectly. Nobody perceives a perfect picture of reality.

There is a pattern to this. We interject our own personalities into what we see and hear. Even when we remember things, we interject our personalities an additional time onto information that was already at least a little wrong. If you have not encountered this already, you will, as long as you are dealing with other stupid people. They will not correctly hear what you said, and they will believe that you said what they expected to hear, instead. This gets worse as they become more distracted by stupid thoughts.

With enough distraction, stupid people can sense very little of the actual world. Irrationality steps in to fill the gaps when someone is too distracted by stupidity to accurately notice the world around them. This is the cause of much stupidity, because information supplied by irrational processes contains far more information about the observer than it contains about the observed.

Chapter 5: You are so stupid that you believe every negative thing describes you

I needed to place this short passage early, even though it contains very abstract information, because it addresses a problem that frequently causes stupid people to read text incorrectly. Many self-condemning stupid people lack self-control when reading feedback, and they greatly overestimate its importance.

In other words, they think that all feedback given to anyone else is also true about them, regardless of accuracy. Their self-heckler is much more skilled than anything else in their minds, and it quickly seizes upon any opportunity to torment these poor stupid people.

This is taken to outlandish extremes, such that even if I complained about people with 5 arms, they would be sure to imagine themselves as being one of those bad people with 5 arms.

Some of the oldest advice from any culture is "know thyself," but these stupid people do not know anything about themselves. Instead, their heads are full of static, with the self-heckler confidently accusing them of outlandish things, most of which cannot possibly be true, much of the rest exaggerated. Cognitive dissonance provides the devil's advocate for anything that can be used against them, and the existence of cognitive dissonance is the only evidence that they require to prove anything negative about themselves.

The driving force behind this is guilt, often hidden under a Fortress of Stupidity. Guilt is powerful. Like most other powerful things, it is highly destructive when used wrongly.

With a head full of ludicrous arguments over whether completely untrue things are true and indicative of worthlessness, the self-condemning stupid person is unlikely to think efficiently. All this static distracts them from more important things that they would be much better off considering. In other words, time is wasted debating obviously untrue things, which become distractions that prevent constructive deliberation.

All this means that you (the self-heckling stupid person) are highly unlikely to properly understand when I am describing stupid thoughts that you actually have. Instead, you will focus on stupid thoughts that you do not have.

Life is tough for people who are constantly and ever-more-creatively falsely accusing themselves and condemning themselves. These unfortunate individuals also habitually overestimate the importance of any other things that manage to catch their attention.

This entire process, when regarding feedback, eventually equalizes the perceived value of all feedback. It reduces the value of useful equal information and puts it on equal footing with the useless. Therefore, all evaluations (regardless of what is actually said) are perceived by these stupid people as being absolutely damning, or as being worthless information supplied by bad people who are judging you, or as being completely inapplicable information for some other reason.

All of this is caused by dysfunctional, self-condemning thoughts that should be identified and dispensed with. Having one stupid person in your head is problem enough, and it can only be made worse by feeding and encouraging a self-heckling element in your mind.

This book can identify many incorrect assumptions made by pointing out some obviously untrue things, but ultimately it is your responsibility and you will fix it or not. You may prize the wrong thoughts kept in your Fortress of Stupidity too much to change it. That would have to be the final word on the matter, because it is not a good idea to fight against the kind of self-destructive determination that causes stupid people to build whole fortresses with their own two hands.

I would add a passage addressing people who have the opposite problem, the belief that every described good quality is a quality that they have, but I do not plan to say a great deal about it. Such people are both happy and cognitively blind. It is even more difficult to get through to them than it is to get through to you, because they are not aware of any reason to change. It is far more likely that you will be here reading about ways to cope with them (despite loving them in one way or another), than it is for them to be reading this in order to seriously help themselves.

Self-condemners are often so unhappy that they may occasionally want to change, but self-flatterers are lost. This is not to say that everyone has a problem in one of these two ways. There are many who do not. I would say that they know who they are, but this is a book for stupid people.

Chapter 6: Cultural worship of stupidity

Some cultures, possibly most or all of them, worship stupidity in one way or another. Some put far more trust in the stupid honest person than in any intelligent person, even though there is no correlation of stupidity with honesty. There is potentially a correlation of stupidity with misunderstanding however, and so this may be a defense mechanism for stupid people. If you do not trust anybody who knows anything, you are also unlikely to be easily tricked by a dishonest person who knows something. You would not need such an elaborate and irrational defense if you were not so stupid.

Chances are that simply becoming smarter would be easier than all of this, but it is occasionally surprising for all of us to realize just how complex the world can be. This is in part because we naturally increase the complexity of our interactions. We increase the complexity of what we expect from others, and we increase the complexity of what we expect from ourselves. The brain may be especially well-suited for this, whether for good or ill.

I may have previously mentioned the impact of stories from entertainment (television, movies, plays, etc.) upon our thought, and it applies here too. It would be staggering and incongruous to the reader if the stupid honest hero of a story failed, because everybody expects honest stupidity to lead to success. Consider how comparatively rare it is to find a story that works as well in praising honest intelligence.

This phenomenon has caused some witty people to build lives around the creation of a stupid but successful entertainment persona. The stupid honest hero has those qualities because they are endearing to the audience, not because they are sure strategies for success. Stupid honesty is not always a bad strategy, but stupid people want to make it the cure for everything as soon as they learn how to use it.

This kind of thing is not new, and it is indeed older than dirt. It goes back far enough that I believe it to be a means of telling stupid people that they are perfectly fine being ignorant of most of the world around them. This may well be true. After all, stupid people should never be asked to solve problems. They are terrible at it, and thereby cause more problems than they solve.

Be happy, ye stupid people, and remember your hero who stumbled backwards into accidental fortune! Just do not try to solve any problems if you are frightfully stupid.

Chapter 7: Stupid people manipulating stupid people

One of the surest ways to become a success is to be excessively but wholeheartedly assured of your superiority, despite all obvious indications otherwise.

This works for many reasons, but if you are a narcissist then at least one person (yourself) loves you, and this can become contagious.

Some especially stupid people need to be told what to do. Some need to feel bad about themselves, or they do not otherwise know what to do and become listless and more conspicuously confused. Such people gravitate towards narcissists, because it confirms their own stupid beliefs about themselves and because it makes them feel a little better if a narcissist occasionally pays some attention to them. This explains the success of some spectacularly stupid narcissists. You know who you are, or maybe you do not but it does not matter.

The primary strategy behind manipulating stupid people is to count on their amazing skill at denying or ignoring truth. They would rather not perceive anything accurately, even at great cost. Stupid people deal with truth like some metaphorical failed archer who rarely hits a target at all, but who claims to be better than those who frequently hit the bullseye. This is well-understood by many, such that people will feel that they know you based on two things: your first reaction to something, and the kinds of incorrect assumptions that you hold.

There is a distinction to be made between manipulation and simpler forms of communication. The goal of simple communication is to convey thoughts, but the goal of manipulation is to guide what others think. Communication can help you consider a variety of thoughts, while manipulation is frequently performed to prevent consideration of alternative thoughts.

Stupid people require someone to either make choices for them, or to let them feel permitted to choose one particular option when they would otherwise not want to think about it. Arguably these are the same thing, but I told it to you in different ways because it manifests in ways that look different.

One of the most terrifying things to the passive, fearful brand of stupid person is the possibility that they will be blamed for a mistake. They go to great lengths to avoid such blame, venturing far into self-destructive territory.

When manipulators such as narcissists intensely and overtly like themselves so much, they tacitly give passive stupid people permission to like them as well. This is a tremendous relief to the poor stupid person who has been quivering in fear for so long while waiting for an obvious option to manifest itself.

This eventually leads to situations that are emotionally or physically abusive. This pattern is so frequent because the evasion of choice can be called an addictive thing, and it is also addictive to push around people who are so desperate to avoid responsibility for their lives.

On the flip side, narcissists absolutely require others to validate their unrealistic self-praise. An absence of people or a presence of disagreeing people will cause narcissists to become visibly desperate because of the strain of maintaining their own Fortress of Stupidity. I do not expect this to be immediately obvious to the reader, not even to the mythical smart one, but I ask you to take a look at people with all of this in mind.

The passive stupid people who are afraid to escape abuse, are also afraid that an attempted escape could be met with crushing disapproval, no matter how much abuse they are receiving right now, no matter how minor and harmless the disapproval could be, and no matter how unlikely the disapproval could be. Any possibility of disapproval is terrifying to them and makes them self-doubt, even if the obvious appropriate response to the disapproval is to throw it back at the disapprover or to otherwise immediately reject it.

I offer some radical ideas to you here. First, abuse is much, much worse than any momentary disapproval. Second, prolonged disapproval coming from within is simply emotional abuse of oneself. Any intense and unforgiving form of disapproval, from within or without, is a form of abuse, and it should not be tolerated.

I am not saying that it is easy to break out of this pattern, but I am saying that I can explain it. I am also saying that it is very rewarding to break out of it and enjoy a balanced and healthy life with rewarding relationships.

Courage is not always easy to have, but it is incumbent upon you to gain it. Others cannot truly give it to you, but if you want: I give you permission to take responsibility for your life. I revoke permission for you to beg others to lead it for you. It may not be fun or easy to gain the courage to ignore inappropriate critique over life choices, much of which comes from within, but a happier and more fulfilled life is the very worthwhile reward.

In case it was not already obvious: manipulation of stupid people requires the effort of more than one individual. The manipulator spends great effort, but potentially an equal amount of effort can be spent in allowing manipulation on a long-term basis. One cannot be manipulated forever without becoming at least mildly aware of it, and this generally requires a Fortress of Stupidity to be built to maintain the situation. Because—well, functional solutions will not do.

But, I digress. You can always count on people to be stupid, and skilled manipulators know this. Like I said (repeated for your benefit because you are stupid), stupid people who feel bad about themselves will always be plentiful because there is a shortage of functional strategies for dealing with guilt. These stupid people provide sustenance and upkeep for manipulators.

People who hate the manipulators because of the obvious lies are also stupid, and so they will fail pitifully. They will look desperate (when in fact you are all desperate), and they will make the manipulator look better. This is because cognitive dissonance will almost always be less prevalent in a manipulator than in any other involved party. The primal perception of cognitive dissonance in anyone who conflicts with the manipulator will be noticed, because of how sharply it contrasts with the lack of apparent cognitive dissonance in the manipulator. This is why we have the term "con-artist."

Attention, regardless of type or intent, always benefits a narcissist. Therefore, if you cannot make a functional choice, choose to be a narcissist instead of being a passive individual or self-condemner. If you are going to be stupid anyway, you should at least be successful because of it. Please note that I will not like you if you are a narcissist, but I also think you are better off being successful than being liked by me. Regardless, a shortage of willing victims will also lead to a shortage of narcissists.

As mentioned earlier, stupid people place great stock in tone of voice, because in some primal way it is trusted, while literal meanings of words are essentially useless. For instance, stupid people will believe that you are the only person in the world with any problems if they hear you complain with feeling. This is why whiners are winners in the land of the stupid.

Stupid people also are far more strongly interested in reactions than in words, because reactions are trusted on a primal level as well. This is why stupid people greatly enjoy following every whim of someone with an entertaining voice and intense reactions. Some skilled stupid people take advantage of this and reach great success by speaking nonsense in an entertaining way and reacting strongly to inconsequential things or inappropriately to consequential things. It takes strong stimulus to penetrate the mind of a stupid person, the more exaggerated the better. Thus, the bizarre false things that stupid people indelibly "learn" by listening and watching such people.

No amount of sensible words, produced in a way not well-designed to entertain, will ever teach a stupid person anything useful. However, nonsense produced in an entertaining voice, or through entertaining reactions, will cause a stupid person to remember something precisely and forever, be it nonsense or sense. This does not work when the actor steps off the stage and speaks simply and out of character. It only works when the actor is acting.

One of the few hopes that boring words have in teaching a stupid person is if the boring words are nonsense, and then some mysterious hook (cognitive dissonance) may cause it to stick in a stupid person's mind, but this is probably not as effective a teacher as entertainment.

Stupid people are highly sensitive to patronizing communication, such that lazy attempts at entertainment sometimes fail miserably. Stupid people believe that they have some special cleverness, E.S.P., or other mysterious insights beyond that of anyone else, and so they demand respect for their intelligence even when they are astoundingly stupid. The effective alternative to patronization is good wit, which is instead one of the best means of convincing stupid people.

There is a rare kind of stupid person who will memorize some boring information that few others know. This is done because this kind of stupid person is somehow aware of their stupidity on some level, and they know that their only hope to sound smart is to dogmatically repeat something that few others know.

Let us call the above-described person the "overspecialized stupid person." This sort of person's stupidity is revealed once any type of departure from rote repetition of their dogma is required in any way. This challenge is usually met by some annoyingly stupid response from this fish out of water, who is very accustomed to being the "big fish" in a very small pond. The most common of these annoyingly stupid responses is to insist that the world exists in a much-reduced state that is oversimplified and grotesquely unrealistic, but which fits in the warped world view of this highly specialized stupid person. Such behavior is tolerated by some pathetic people, but it should be tolerated by nobody.

The overspecialized stupid person is seen as an authority by some other stupid people (because they believe only in absolutes and are far too lazy to know anything), but some understand that information from an overspecialized stupid person is no more inherently reliable than that provided by anyone else. Smart people verify any information that is important, but this is rarely done, because people are stupid.

I am not sure if I pointed it out directly enough above, but dogmatism is an intensely stupid method used by stupid people who have no hope of figuring out anything on their own. This does not stop dogmatic stupid people. To be fair, dogma does have a purpose, but stupid people like to misuse it. The purpose of dogma is to enhance memorization and speed of information retrieval.

If something is never questioned, it does not need to take up extra space in a state of simultaneous "correctness" and "incorrectness" as cognitive dissonance until resolved. Remember that stupid people rarely resolve anything in their minds. This means that information takes up far less space in their minds for their entire lives if they dogmatically accept everything that they want to know. This saved space is spent on the endless repetition of useless thoughts that are typically self-destructive.

Consider that computers can only use dogmatic methods, always assuming their stored information to be true. When was the last time that your computer worked right?

Dogmatic stupid people are always scanning their world for information that can be internalized as dogma. This includes opinions. For the dogmatic stupid person, opinions are either absolutely and immutably right, or absolutely and irreconcilably wrong. To them there is no bad in a dogmatically accepted opinion, and no good in a rejected one. There is no such thing as an "acceptable" opinion, nor one that is merely "good enough" to a dogmatist, who deals only in absolutes and never in degrees. This contradicts reality, because every opinion has at least a little connection to truth, and at least a little inaccuracy in it.

A smart person would take a useful-enough opinion, refine it until they are happy with it, and re-use it or re-evaluate it as purposes dictate. To the dogmatist, an accepted opinion is only an endpoint never to be improved.

A subjective and partially inaccurate opinion can have the same undeniability to the dogmatist as the fact that two plus two equals four. A dogmatist uses facts and dogmatically accepted opinions in the same ways: as building blocks for their Fortresses of Stupidity.

A too-inaccurate opinion can be like a poorly selected or poorly hewn stone, producing a bad foundation and weakening the "building" that is a belief system. Thoughts are not entirely like stones, however, which is part of what the dogmatist does not understand. Thoughts can be easily converted into modular things of different granularity, removed from the foundation without toppling the "building," and re-shaped without necessarily weakening connections with other ideas. Smart people do this. Dogmatic people do not.

Even though dogmatists are suboptimal thinkers, I feel that it is a bad idea to try to change the mind of a dogmatist and open their minds to the whole concept of modular thought. The minds of dogmatists are shaped around the entire concept that informational change is bad. They are possibly better left that way, because it would be a pitiful state of affairs if dogmatic stupid people were given the job of refining and improving upon opinions. The resulting chaos could destroy much. Leave the job of thinking to the smart people, and the job of remembering to the dogmatists, and do not try to mix their roles.

Chapter 8: Politics is stupid, including yours

You can always count on politics to result in many stupid people calling each other stupid. Despite always being correct about this, they occasionally manage to foul it up, in part because they think that only others are stupid and that they are not.

Political stupid people blame those in opposed parties when things go wrong, because being honest about mistakes can only supply ammunition to stupid opponents. And we know that some people never make mistakes, right? It removes the mystique of it all if your political hero makes an admitted mistake, because you are stupid enough to wholeheartedly believe in personal infallibility to such an extreme degree that only an infallible person is acceptable.

Only a fundamentally dishonest person would try to maintain the obviously false impression of a mistake-free life just to help you maintain enough laziness and stupidity to vote for them. This is why you cannot have nice things.

In case the above did not spell it out clearly enough, the point of politics is to blame everything on someone else. Additionally, being in a political party does not grant you a hating license, but stupid people think it does. A person's chosen political beliefs simply guide the blame to a consistent target and codify the blame system such that a stupid person can rant to similar stupid people without generating confusion.

Opposing parties are disliked not because they differ in policy, but because of simple personal dislike of those in opposing parties. Different political systems result in blaming those of a particular race, religion, background, geographical location, educational level, or some other trait from among a vast list of hated traits. And yes, if you are "defined" by anything, then a given political party will arbitrarily like or hate you for it.

Blaming everything on one highly restricted set of stupid people is a stupid thing to do, in part because it is a very lazy approach where people do not exercise their skills to figure things out functionally. Without exercising discernment skills, stupid people never realize how useful it is to examine reality with a properly granular view. That is, stupid people "paint" everything with ideological brush strokes that are far too broad. Thus, every political discussion is full of lazy rants that have little or nothing to do with what a reasonable person would think.

Political discussion mainly serves to relieve the stress caused by one's own cognitive dissonance, instead of being an actual attempt at communication with others. If anything, rationality is a minus where political success is concerned, because stupid people believe that any rational person is too weak to become properly radicalized. And make no mistake: radicalization is what parties want. You can count on radicals to vote for you, when a rational person could end up voting for someone else.

The more stupid you are, the more you need politics and the more important it becomes to you. This is because politics is a crutch, serving to codify a set of stupid beliefs into something that may get votes from large numbers of stupid people.

Politics guides stupid people into selecting what they can properly rant about or praise in order to be liked by people who are important to them. If you and others were smart, you would be able to think on your own, and you would not need a code of stupid beliefs or some other stupid person to tell you what to think or do.

Politics has the power to make anything true or false. Indeed, facts do not matter in the politics of stupid people: in a world where nothing makes sense, there is no meaningful distinction between fact and falsehood. There are a few different ways to disseminate political ideas, but the news, social media, and public clubs are among the current accepted avenues for this. All of these avenues naturally veer towards increased radicalization. What happens to the comedian who does not tell jokes? That same thing will happen to a news service that does not induce outrage.

When politics becomes extremely important to many stupid people, they murder each other, because murder starts seeming like a good idea at that stage of radicalization. If these people were smart, they would know that friends, family, and productive lives are more important than stupid beliefs about things that they do not understand, but people are stupid and therefore they do not know this.

On a smaller scale, stupid people will assume that disagreement is a form of competition, and that to disagree is to accuse. At no point will they welcome the idea that a resolution could depart from "both" sides of the discussion. This is in part because the real topic on people's minds may go completely without mention in a political discussion. There are vast numbers of surrogate issues, all forming an onion-like Fortress of Stupidity around the real goal of a party.

The reason that your political beliefs are stupid is that you try to make them too simplistic and try to apply them to situations where they do not adequately solve problems. Yet, you will demand in a radicalized way that your stupid answer is the best one because it belongs to your stupid party.

Politics is invariably filled with desperate and fundamentally dishonest people who will do anything to spread their stupid beliefs. Some people, despite their stupidity, eventually catch on that these desperate and dishonest people are not entirely on the up-and-up, and this generates political opposition. This is why every major political party generates a set of opponents roughly equal to its supporters in number, radicalization, and stupidity. Some might call this yin and yang, but it is simply stupid people behaving stupidly.

Many radicalized stupid people believe that all of reality revolves around one issue. This is not always a bad thing, but it is always an annoying thing. The good of it occurs when it results in a positive change in laws. Stupid people are highly resistant to changing their minds, and so having a viewpoint repeated to them loudly by large numbers of irate people may be about the only way to bring about any lasting political change. I have not seen any lasting political change derive solely from rational discussion. A few changes may originate from the efforts of some poor rational individual, but lasting change would occur only after radicalized people get hold of it and turn it into a highly altered slogan that even stupid people can remember. It also helps if things rhyme, or if you can make demeaning caricatures of all your opponents.

When a topic becomes political, it immediately generates supporters and opponents that are about equal in number, as said earlier. It does not matter if the message on one or both sides is obviously true or false: supporters and opponents will appear. Indeed, the word "obvious" loses all literal meaning in politics. For this reason, politics tends to perpetuate debate and does not solve many problems.

Most of the good in the world is done despite politics, not because of it. Yet, even an evil such as politics has a use: it gets political debate out in the open, so that we can feel what it is like to be for or against an issue while facing opposition. Even though it is usually tiresome, political debate can lead to progress that would not be otherwise achievable or even apparent as a possibility.

Any political issue that miraculously escapes being politicized, to become universally resolved, will also become boring. Controversial topics will supplant it in the minds of party members. That is, unless someone decides that they want to exercise their debating skills through defending the undefendable. We are usually so terrible at defending the obvious, that the person fervently defending the undefendable will prove to be more fascinating in the "minds" of the stupid public.

You will probably not find many who can tell you exactly what their party is about, if they belong to a larger or older party. Instead, they will tell you the issues of the day, or rants about another party, without connection to what their party stands for. It is difficult to break through all of that to emerge into a real discussion. This is in part why people without much political awareness cannot easily make political decisions. Choosing a party is not difficult when information is complete, but it becomes difficult when all sides are irate. This is not to say that calm and informative behavior will win the day. Much the opposite actually, because calm people do not get attention.

The existence of a minor or mostly disliked party will also draw some stupid people to it, because we cannot be happy with simply having good things. Opportunistic, but lazy, people also realize that they have a better chance of advancing with bad ideas that are well-known and enthusiastically communicated. If we were smart, we would immediately perceive this and prevent these lazy people from having political power, but we are not smart.

Because stupid people tend to reward desperation, and because so many people are so stupid, desperate people with conspicuously bad ideas gain far more power than they should. The attention gained by this can be intoxicating, leading to rapid radicalization. Possibly this could be prevented if there were more rewards for people who are not desperate, but unfortunately resources such as attention are limited (that is, hogged up by a few desperate greedy people) and therefore stupid people must rely upon desperation to help gain what they stupidly believe they deserve.

Politics is full of people who want impossible things, including things that seem very reasonable, but which have never existed anywhere. An example is how many ask for "unity" as if it is something that they need, that some society once had. The dream of unity is an impossible will o' the wisp. It has never existed. If there is apparent unity, it is because some are not saying what they really think, are not thinking, or are silently not getting what they want. We are contentious beings, never exactly agreeing but sometimes working together despite disagreement. Unity has not been lost, but maturity has been lost.

I will add something now that would devastate the political world if it was widely understood: complete certainty over an idea does not accompany a strong emotional need to have it validated. People do not scream, "Hell yeah!" whenever we see 2+2=4. This is not because simple addition has a lack of impact. It is because nobody has serious doubt over it. There is no tension when 2+2=? appears for anyone who has graduated up to multiplication tables. There is no relief upon discovering that you are speaking to a fellow 2+2=4 supporter.

If instead you said, "My stance on politics is..." there would be at least a little tension, because everyone knows on some level that every political topic encounters some active disagreement. This potential disagreement generates tension even when we want to be as certain as possible. A heightened emotional state is gained whenever the topic comes to mind, and this is why politics does not lead to complete agreement. Complete agreement does not even occur within one's own mind, as shown by the presence of cognitive dissonance.

Subjective issues are easy to throw into political controversy, but even obvious facts can become political. When obvious facts become political, they stop being universally perceived as obvious. The 2+2=5 supporters will increase in fervor and the 2+2=4 supporters will respond with similar zeal. The conflict will proceed to generate tension in everyone.

Any supposedly controversial fact stops being obvious at that point, and it becomes a keyword that generates conflict even within the minds of supporters. It is not necessarily the case that we will intellectually doubt that 2+2=4, but we will constantly be self-reminded that those who believe that 2+2=5 are not always so completely wrong about other topics. They can, for instance, dress themselves and do other activities that should require them to know the simplest arithmetic, regardless of what they say that they believe.

Additionally, politicization of a topic ensures that it will not be resolved, barring violence or some miracle. The 2+2=5 supporters will not go away once they become radicalized. They will not stop, not even if you make them count on their fingers. They will reject your other opinions, and will reject you personally, because they disagree with your arithmetic. They will train new generations of arithmetic deniers who will eventually come into power once the topic becomes sufficiently muddled by controversy.

The outrage over a controversial issue may be due to disbelief that the issue is controversial, but some inner doubt will be present, or no tension would be generated. This reveals part of the power of politics to generate large scale conflict. The emotion going into opposition of an obvious fact helps generate the controversy. A few people do understand this, and they use it to their advantage politically by controlling public focus on a topic. There is good strategy in doing this, because some people are poorly skilled at defending anything. There can be considerable disbelief over how an obvious fact has become political, which leads to it being defended without appropriate conviction. This yields victory to those who only know how to emotionally oppose obvious facts.

Chapter 9: Scientists are stupid and smart all at the same time

You are stupid enough to believe that labels define a person, and therefore that the word "scientist" somehow defines a smart person. This is a similar mentality to the stupid idea that the "clothing makes the man," when in reality clothing makes a deceit or fantasy (or some kind of protection, but who really uses clothing for that?). This labeling fetish says far more about your own stupidity than it does about the people who are labeled.

Many of you stupid people are cheering at the idea that scientists (and therefore science) are stupid. You are doing this while watching your television, waiting for someone to deliver something to you with their automobile or airplane, and probably benefiting from some recently discovered medication. In other words, your hypocrisy is comical, and you are just as stupid as the scientists, possibly more so, but that would be staggering to comprehend.

The point of this chapter is to indicate that science, despite the soundness of the scientific method, is just as much a platform of miserable stupidity as any other part of human life. Instead of making scientific advances, most scientists waste time and money arguing pointlessly with each other and with other stupid people over trivialities. This is sometimes called "workplace management," but scientists are generally too stupid to know what that means. A V.I.P. scientist can be just as horrible as any other V.I.P., and dishonest, greedy scientists have been around for almost the exact length of time that science has existed. Anything that people trust in any way will be hijacked by greedy people, including science.

And yes, no stupid people, not even stupid scientists, like the scientific method. The whole point of the scientific method is to guide investigation by use of a structured framework for testing hypotheses. However, stupid people do not like guidance because guidance involves direction and restrictions. They want to concoct whatever conclusion makes them happiest without having to arrive at it through any structured method.

Stupid people do not understand direction. They want to arrive at point Z from point A without ever considering points B through Y. Stupid people also redefine words into whatever suits them at the moment, and therefore what they mean by "hypothesis" is an ever-changing thing that rarely coincides with what anyone influential in development of the scientific method had meant by the word.

The entire process of structured investigation is alien to stupid people, who rely entirely upon stupid brands of intuition. Yet, every stupid person wants to give their stupid ideas the legitimacy that is bestowed by arbitrarily labeling them as "scientifically proven results." Never mind that the scientific method does not result in proof, but in rejection of alternatives. Such complications get in the way of all-important gut instincts.

If we had time machines, we would probably immediately destroy ourselves. However, in the unlikely event that it was impossible to destroy ourselves, we would soon realize that we would have been laughed out of the room in any 19th Century scientific society if we ever said much about what we knew of science. This is in part because everyone involved (including ourselves) is stupid, but it is also because the 19th Century scientific community "knew" many things that would make modern life impossible.

Such is the case with cliques of all sorts, including scientific ones. Acceptance in a clique entails accepting their nonsense even more than it entails accepting their sense. This is because anybody can agree with sensible ideas, but it takes dedication to accept nonsense.

I do not wish to bash scientists too much, because most of them are miserable people competing for the same pittance ($3.50). Additionally, everyone, including other scientists, dislike and disbelieve all scientific work except for a small amount of what was done by dead people.

Some may say that they like work done by another living scientist, but this is a lie told to help maintain funding at $3.50 instead of letting it be reduced to $3.49. Just consider one thing: there are some scientists who will cut your throat over that $3.50. This distinguishes them from businessmen, for instance, who will usually not bother cutting a throat for less than six figures.

The most frequent complaints from stupid non-scientists are that science is boring, false, or irritating in some poorly specified way. In reality, science is disliked because it conflicts with cherished but stupid beliefs, or because somebody else wanted the $3.50 that funded the work.

Teachers have no idea how science, mathematics, education, or anything else works, which increases the boredom when they try to teach it. Scientists get paid $3.50 to tell you that some things are not true, which makes them widely disliked. Meanwhile, politicians, entertainers, and so forth, get paid millions to deliberately lie to you. Many of you have probably made the connection between those two statements by now, but if not, here it is: many stupid people hate science because it challenges their modes of entertainment.

Stupid people believe all kinds of wrong things because it keeps them from being bored. As they turn wrongness into an ingrained habit, they gain camaraderie with others who are also wrong.

They find it interesting to tweak their minds by playing with the slight emotional thrill that goes along with skirting the edges of conspiracy theories and other lies.

Goodness knows that stupid people cannot possibly do anything else besides wallow in wrongness as a response to boredom. They could not, for instance, do something interesting as a hobby, which would be laughably unacceptable. Instead, they want to endlessly self-amuse by tossing about wrong things as if they were facts.

Stupid people want to keep their cherished lies around forever, constantly bringing them up and hinting that they could be true. False statements are deliberately not resolved, because they can be at least slightly fun. Science barges in to shut that down by saying once and for all that some statements are just not true, and this gets the same reception that someone preaching prohibition would get at a pub.

This is not to say that the endpoints of science, such as discoveries, nice photographs, and confident speeches about results, are disliked. Much to the contrary, such things are well-liked in all fields because they are very useful for manipulating stupid people. However, any sound and robust means of reaching these endpoints, such as adherence to the scientific method and attention to details, is disliked.

Stupid people, including stupid scientists, would much rather rush to fun endpoints. This is true for all things that people do, because stupid people hate to wait for quality results, wagering that verification is a useless waste of time. One reason for this wager is the danger that some disreputable scientist (and only a scientist can be "disreputable" in this goofy language) will scoop them by reporting the same stupid conclusions earlier than someone who did any data quality control. Therefore, the favored amount of quality control, in the upper echelon of science, is zero.

Very few people ever verify data, and they always get in trouble with their bosses. In short, quality control feels like a wonderful thing to some, but it feels like a dumb thing immediately after someone scoops you.

Stupid people believe that "faster" is better than "more reliable," thus the vast amount of quickly developed, unreliable products emerging from all fields, science included. Stupid scientists generally will report inaccurate results with extreme confidence, and then they will inconspicuously retract incorrect results once they get caught reporting wrong things. This is because they know that you are stupid. The ones who qualify what they say, who express reasonable doubt over preliminary results, or who do not speak with excessive confidence, are pushed out of the field, are given even less than $3.50, and are perceived as weak and deeply conflicted individuals.

Many other problems are caused by stupid scientists who believe that one person is inherently more reliable than another, without requiring sufficient information to verify statements. Never mind that it is not science if someone involved is too important to be wrong or too unimportant to be right.

Thinking is hard, even for scientists, and nobody is going to think if they do not have to. It is through mistaken adherence to personal infallibility that many stupid assumptions are perpetuated and converted into dogma, simply because some famous stupid scientist said it.

Ideally, assumptions would be stated in a structured way, and hypotheses tested, but this would make the whole thing even more boring to stupid people, such that some of them may die from the boredom of reading it. This would not seem to be such a bad result, except that it could cause a stampede from all the other stupid people who witness such a piteous death. Stupid people are slow to pick up on many things, but they are quick to perceive when something kills their own kind.

The only saving grace of science is that nobody (including other scientists) has any idea what is published in any scientific work. To stupid people, one misleading scientific result is a rejection of all science. Never mind that there are some misleading results in all endeavors. Stupid people believe in all or nothing, and so one admitted error is to them tantamount to rejection of an entire field.

An exception to the above is if they approve of a field for arbitrary reasons, and then no amount of mistakes can make them change their minds. This is especially the case if politics is involved, because politics can make anything true or false. In such cases, stupid people will instead decide that they must believe everything instead of nothing. Belief is not supposed to play a part in this, but remember that we are talking about stupid people here. Belief is all that they have. Rationality plays no part in their lives, and they do not know how to deal with "some." It is all or nothing to them.

Chapter 10: Religious people are stupid, bless their souls

Many of you stupid people will only like this section or the previous one, not both. However, both of those stances are incredibly stupid.

Religion is full of people who lie, steal, murder, covet their neighbor's ass, touch poop without permission, eat the wrong things, and so forth. They are not any better than the scientists, even though they will tell you that they are.

Sometimes religious stupid people will hide their disdain for you by "blessing" you or allegedly fearing for your soul, but this all means hideous things when translated into anyone else's words.

Some will say that their religion does not conflict with science, but they are doubly stupid. Religion and religious people inadvertently teach us that stupidity is not exceptionally new or different. They will tell you that a dead or immaterial being either loves you or told you to do and/or not do random things, and that you should give them money. This will somehow be comforting, because you are stupid.

All this aside, the purpose of religion is to tell you who to hate. I said something like this about politics as well, and it was true there too. Stupid people need to be told all kinds of things, but it seems to be deeply important to tell them who to hate.

Just listen to religious people for a while. If someone is different from them, and their religion says it is all right to hate in this instance, they will hate with extreme zeal. Ask them to accept someone who is different, and they will be at least a little reluctant no matter what their religion says. Similar things are true for every clique. Cliques are defined by cultural traits rather than by ideas, but this is more conspicuous where religion is concerned.

Look at the people who are telling you how and why you should worship. Most of them are immaculately dressed and apparently rich. I think they use some kind of spray plastic to make themselves look shiny, but maybe their deities provide something that is about the same as spray plastic. A few endeavor to look poor, depending on the religion, but they try to outcompete each other in this respect, thereby voiding whatever they said about spirituality. There is little substantial difference between people who try to look richer than the other preacher, versus those who try to have fewer attachments than some other guru. Both are competing in petty ways that make their religions look dumb.

There are many different religions, but all of them are stupid and are mainly distinguished by how they torture themselves and others. A secondary purpose of religion is to make you feel like you are better than others, but some forbid you to say this. Many religions establish that even getting to a comfy afterlife is a competitive process, and that only a few people will earn a spot in the allegedly limited seating of this non-physical place. Others open the door wide for all sorts of miserably stupid and bad people, but this is only done to increase donations.

Religious people murder and are murdered by those who have different religions and different numbers of worshippers and weapons. This is especially frequent in religions that tell their followers to not murder. Some allegedly peaceful stupid people simply insult others in different religions instead of murdering them, but this is rare. The aforementioned murdering is done supposedly because they differ in beliefs, but none of them has any idea what their holy scriptures say. In reality, the murdering is done because they hate one another, and basing it on what some stupid theologian says is an obviously false pretext that is intended to make murder look justified.

Religious hypocrisy is a well-known phenomenon, even though everyone is a hypocrite. This highlights how being good is a boring thing that anyone could do if it was not so boring, while becoming well-known as a bad person in a religious setting takes creativity and is exciting. This is because you are stupid. Your special religion is also stupid, and you are not better than the infidels, idolaters, unbelievers, atheists, and other stupid people who differ from you only in that they do not believe the same stupid thing that you do. Your religion may have changed your life, but you are still a stupid hypocrite and you have no idea what your holy book (or scroll, or verbal tradition) says.

It is a bad thing for stupid people to actually know what their scriptures say, because it confuses them and makes the communicate with less conviction. A confused stupid person is a very hopeless thing, which is exactly the opposite of what their religion was supposed to do for them. It is much easier and more effective for them to latch onto some false stupid idea arbitrarily than to look it up. Some stupid people may differ by becoming dogmatic and only relying upon looking things up, which is similar to wearing a "stupid" sign for all others to see.

Religions generally contain vast numbers of bizarrely wrong statements which hide a few useful statements that have defied the odds to survive this long. Simply put, goofy stories are more fun than simple facts.

Entertainment has an extreme effect upon the focuses of religion. Heroic religious figures are remembered for their feats. Villainous religious figures are remembered for their schemes. Stupid people require simple stories, and therefore badness tends to be portrayed as ugly, while goodness is portrayed as beautiful. This leads stupid people to conclude that bad or evil things are always ugly, and that beautiful people are always good. In reality, there is no manipulator who will not try to look impeccably good. Would you really believe someone who has horns and a pointy tail? If so, you have more problems than I can solve.

What we call "spiritual health" is a very misunderstood thing. It is the result of deeper moods that function in ways that are at least a little different from what we usually call emotions. Even those who have no religious beliefs have this kind of health, and therefore it is not truly spiritual in the religious sense. Let us make up a new term for it and get it away from these hypocrites. Mood health improves when you think that you have done good things without causing harm, experienced the impossible such as revisiting a good past event, or other such things. It decays when we experience guilt, shame, or other emotions that are mostly perceived as negative.

Nothing is entirely positive or negative, and anything can be used properly or misused. We all need outlets to make us forget events that induce guilt and shame, and these are what promote mood health and reject some types of despondency.

People need some kind of outlet to help favorably answer questions such as "will my mistakes and inadequacies prevent me from ever being a real adult." We also arguably need means of upgrading our own self-perception from childhood to adulthood, which is what rites of passage once frequently did. Rites once widely helped stupid people absolve guilt and shame, but we have gradually moved away from rites as we have become aware of how much more destruction we can cause with non-ritualized technology. It is tough to make stupid people listen, and they tend to stop listening if you cannot destroy them.

Many modern societies could use some new ways to convince stupid people to reject guilt and shame. Instead, stupid people go all or nothing: rejecting the possibility of changing mood, or dwelling on spirituality all the time and thereby decreasing its power to improve anything.

Chapter 11: Philosophers are stupid too, but nobody cares or exists

I felt like this needed to be said, but I am sure that no philosopher will understand it or like it. It is always a plus to anger philosophers anyway, as they all will tell you in one way or another. At least they like it when you make another philosopher angry, even if they do not like it when you make them angry.

Philosophers are the last people to ever realize any important thing. They then write these things down, so that other abysmally stupid people can supposedly read them later. This would be quite viable if only anyone could wade through massive amounts of useless philosophical statements that hide anything of value. Nevertheless, humanity can only progress when rational thought catches up to right things that we "know" emotionally and rejects wrong things that we also "know."

Friedrich Nietzsche is known mainly for writing that God is dead. This may be true inasmuch as a non-physical thing could live or die, but philosophy is just as dead regardless. Truth died at some point or another and could not be deader. It is very possible that stupidity killed them all, because stupidity has survived this massacre while thriving and growing.

Even if you have the best ideas of all time, it will not help you, because your ideas will surpass the vision of anyone who could ever invest in you or believe in you. While your own capabilities may not hold you back, other people are very much capable of doing so. It is therefore far more important, in terms of success, to have timely ideas than to have the best ones. This explains why so many philosophers waste so much time on nonsense. Success often requires you to understand and accept the wrong things that many other stupid people believe at a given moment.

Some stupid people with a memory (these may not exist) may point out that philosophy has provided an alternative to extreme-oriented thinking by providing a Golden Mean or a Doctrine of the Mean. For you stupid people out there, it means a perfect middle between extremes. I would be all for this, except that stupid people have ruined it already by focusing on an impossibly small ideal midpoint. This indicates the infinite power of stupidity: it can even turn a midpoint into an extreme.

To name something is to reject it in the minds of many allegedly learned stupid people. "That is x-ism and therefore invalid," they will say. They will not tell you why it is invalid, because stupid people do not use actual reasoning. Therefore, the worst thing that can ever happen to you is to be labeled. Nobody will listen to you after that. Beware of those who have a labeling gun.

Some philosophers deny knowing everything that all the others have finally realized. Therefore, the purpose of being the last person to realize something is not upheld by them. These know-nothing philosophers are even more useless than the others. Everything they write is only good for mocking other philosophers and themselves, and they are only tolerated because they are sometimes mocking someone that others would also like to mock.

Philosophers are also among the first to "realize" any unimportant or untrue thing, but most people already knew this despite being stupid. It does not matter if an allegedly new idea "discovered" by a philosopher (we know better than that) is important or not, because nobody will ever read it.

Chapter 12: All the humanities are just as stupid as the humans

The humanities are in a difficult position in academia, in that they must continuously justify their worth but are mainly distinguished by how thoroughly humanities professors have read, seen, or listened to something that nobody else has read, seen, or heard. Therefore, we must take their word for it all.

Long centuries of this pattern have led humanities experts to become similar to lawyers in that they must be convincing above all, and need not have integrity. After all, anybody can claim to have thought about some book, piece of art, or music, but nobody will check up on it, because research is painful for stupid people and none of them have time for it. Even if stupid people somehow go to the trouble of trying to research something, they will still not resolve the question even after long years of trying.

If any humanities professors actually did produce something of value, all the others would become jealous and force them out of the field. Eventually this teaches stupid people that they should never research, and that they are better off blindly guessing, trolling, or leaving decisions up to some other stupid person. You could write that Charles Dickens predicted the invention of computers, and nobody will ever be able to show that you are wrong, because who the hell reads all of Charles Dickens' books today? Since there is strong pressure for humanities professionals to have new ideas, many of them will provide "new," but ultimately unsupportable, interpretations of old works.

All this leads many humanities professionals to become starved for attention and increasingly desperate. Such stupid people are likely to become political apologists, professional trolls, or philosophers who only ostensibly study the humanities. Saying something vacuous but exciting to today's stupid people is far more effective in making them relevant enough to keep a job, after all. This is far more effective than accurately interpreting some old text that nobody except them has read in centuries, because stupid people have never heard of this text.

Still, there may be a small handful on Earth at a given time who are competent to interpret old texts. This job should be left to them, instead of giving it to those who can only dish out useless statements about modern-day topics. There is no shortage of stupid people who want to go on blathering forever about modern topics, and therefore such people should not be paid.

I include all sociopolitical parts of social science in the same category as humanities, because they are all just humanities people and they know it. You can spout crap for only so long before the whole world, even the stupid people, calls you out on it. Once even the stupid people know that you are stupid, there is no longer much hope of reversing perceptions.

Chapter 13: Things that you do not know anything about, which bother you anyway

Being stupid, you know very little. However, you speculate stupidly about many things. Whenever you supposedly know something, no matter how false it is, you will most likely use it to torture yourself for no good reason.

We fear many things that are impossible or unlikely, gaining strong beliefs about things that we know nothing about. The less that is known, the stronger the belief, because expressing something with greater conviction makes it more accurate in the supposed mind of a stupid person. The whole process of self-delusion is derailed in the presence of inconvenient but accurate knowledge.

Stupid people are bothered by many things that are unimportant and untrue, but cognitive dissonance causes them to continuously consider these things as if they had some possibility of being true. This is especially frequent among self-condemning stupid people, who are always looking for some excuse to make themselves feel bad. You probably have seen this happen before. Someone will feel accused, even when nobody is insinuating anything. Or, possibly an unclear but innocent sentence becomes misinterpreted as a nasty insult about the supposed ugliness of one of their body parts.

Stupid people believe that hidden messages exist in every sentence, and nothing can convince them that you ever say anything that does not conceal things that you are afraid to say directly. This can lead these poor stupid people to completely miss when you say very plainly what you want or do not want. They may assume that you want things that you do not want, or that you want exactly the same things that they want. Such stupid people are hopelessly lost within their Rat Tunnels and may not have fully noticed another person in years.

These wrong assumptions about supposedly unvoiced desires will reveal subtle details that describe the mindset of a stupid person. For instance, bad people expect that everyone else is also bad, concluding that the weak have reason to hide it. This makes bad stupid people readily identifiable through their assumption that everyone else has corrupt motives, and through their lack of understanding that anyone could be actually good.

A much happier life can be had without clumsily misinterpreting vague parts of other people's sentences. We do not truly need to project ourselves onto everything that we read and hear.

As another example, only a truly bad individual would say the horrible things that are anticipated by the self-condemning stupid person. A person saying such horrible things should be judged far more harshly than you. It is perfectly fine to revoke someone's permission to be horrible. Still, cruel people are so frequent that a very large number of self-hecklers believe that verbal abuse is normal or even some sort of attractive honesty. Self-hecklers are therefore to be pitied but their permission to self-heckle should be revoked.

Let me indulge in an aside on the acceptance of bad ways of living. Acceptance is clearly something in limited supply. Many innocent people are downright hated for no good reason. Why not revoke your acceptance and love for cruel people, so that you have more to spare for those who actually deserve it?

The self-condemning stupid person may wish for others to take control of social interactions, to inject energy or disperse blame. However, others are not always up to this challenge, because they have lives of their own. Please consider that an honest person may not always be prepared to inject energy into every occasion, but a dishonest person is usually prepared for any opportunity to manipulate. You will have a more fulfilled life if you learn how to be comfortable with your own social interactions at your own pace, instead of relying upon being energized by others who may not be working in your best interests.

Stupid people torture themselves by worrying about misunderstood things in undisciplined ways. This is sometimes a sign of (again) self-condemnation in the form of guilt or regret, such as when family members worry about absent relatives but do not properly interact with them when they reunite.

Other stupid people worry themselves into a panic when faced with any possibility of well-characterized harm, such as when they take an airplane flight. Never mind that crashes are rare, the misplaced attention on the possibility of a crash drives them. And again: "rare" has zero reality in the mind of a stupid person. Rare is either always or never to them, not indicating some frequency near zero.

Movies and television, our great teachers, have great influence upon the creation of rehearsed responses that shape misguided fears, but it goes beyond that.

Stupid people very frequently re-enact mistakes that they have seen portrayed in entertainment. Some will collide with you when you are carrying coffee, for instance, but they would not collide with your hand in the same situation. They expect coffee collisions to be less avoidable than hand collisions, because they have "witnessed" coffee collisions more often in movies and television and expect them on an underlying level.

Similar examples exist in a vast number of situations. Much of the education from movies and television works in this way: fully accepted but not necessarily consciously referenced. This makes such education undeniable in the so-called minds of stupid people.

Plane crashes in entertainment inspire the conclusion that crashes are far more frequent than is really the case. Portrayals and sounds associated with animals on television will cause stupid people to believe that some animals are more dangerous or friendly than they actually are. Portrayals of actors who have a certain appearance will lead us to indelibly conclude that everyone who looks like those actors will be the same as their characters on the screen. We all know that fiction is fiction, but few of us know that fictional portrayals are completely unreliable indicators of anything.

Chapter 14: You are stupid because you fail to evaluate anything properly

This may be a difficult point to get across, but I am making the attempt anyway. Each stupid person tends to believe that they are fundamentally different from all other people. This stupid idea is understandable but can be expanded to an absurd and damaging extent, mainly to spectacularly fail at evaluating oneself or another stupid person.

Believing in absolutes, stupid people generally assume that they are either absolutely perfect or absolutely failed, and/or that some other person differs in being absolutely failed or absolutely perfect. Being impossible but opposite absolutes, the states of failed and perfect are treated as mutually exclusive, and therefore the "perfect" person is unconditionally praised and the "failed" person is unconditionally condemned.

This type of evaluation is always grossly inaccurate, because none of us is absolutely good or bad. Even though stupid people may intend this as a shortcut, reducing thoughts-per-day and saving valuable brain-space for the entertaining repetition of stupid self-destructive thoughts, it saves no actual time and simply results in greater inconvenience for all of us.

Much consternation results from the stupid assumption that some apparently happy person, who "has it all" and is respected by others, is perfect. This person therefore becomes simultaneously a goal and unattainable.

Each of us is, at least subconsciously but sometimes consciously, aware of some of our own mistakes or flaws, and therefore the supposed existence of this perfect other person becomes extremely stressful. After all, being inherently and irreversibly flawed, we can never become perfect and compete with perfect individuals, right? Such are the self-destructive and completely bogus thoughts that fly around in the head of many stupid people, causing needless anxiety and troubles.

Many false assumptions were needed to reach this state of conceptual disaster, and they can work together synergistically to produce a Fortress of Stupidity. It can be difficult to decide which of these inaccurate assumptions is a highly vulnerable section of the fortress wall that is best destroyed first, such that sensible thoughts can eventually enter and leave one's mind again, but let us try.

First of all, nobody is perfect. This gets repeated endlessly but somehow is not convincing, just as many other obvious things are boring and unconvincing. Some people may appear to be perfect, and this is because they have reached an apparently "finished" stage in some professional or social progression. This is not perfection in an absolute sense, but we need to spend extra effort to prove this to ourselves.

The word "perfect" originated as a word for "finished," and we can misuse this information to our advantage. What may have appeared to be perfect centuries or millennia ago, would today be rejected as wholly inadequate. A "perfect-looking" person from that long ago would be considered merely one among many moderately attractive people today. The lice would be a major problem, however, as would the complete lack of bathing with soap.

When self-condemning stupid people consider the "perfect," they are daunted by someone who has gotten to a certain apparently finished stage through an unknown amount of effort and unknown means. Because stupid people use unrealistic and grossly inaccurate assumptions whenever they guess at an unknown quantity, they tend to assume that the process of reaching "perfection" was effortless, instantaneous, or otherwise semi-mystical.

In reality, there is always a great deal of work and effort spent to bring anyone to a prominent stage of accomplishment.

Sometimes this effort was not spent entirely by the "perfect person." Sometimes it required good help from capable friends, for instance, because the allegedly perfect people believed in themselves so much that it became contagious.

The best response upon learning all this is for you, too, to believe in yourself, at least to a realistic extent. Most certainly it is very stupid to self-condemn, and you will not gain anything from being in a constant state of despair simply because someone else is successful. Once again, if you insist on being wrong about yourself, try to be wrong in a way that helps you. Just consider that one reason that you do not have nice things, is because you may be spending far too much time fretting over how someone else allegedly has nice things.

Through appropriately believing in yourself and in your potential, you help teach others how to believe in you. If you condemn yourself, you teach others how to condemn you. Consider that other people are stupid too. They need as much help as they can get. Be willing to give them a crutch if necessary.

Nobody is happy all of the time. We are actually incapable of being happy all of the time, at least when our body's systems are running properly. One frequent response from people who have all of their needs met, is to become despondent for no reason that they can specify. People therefore seem to need challenges in order to be happy. In other words, the best part of achieving a goal is the process of getting there, not simply the reward upon reaching the goal. This may bring to mind something that you may not have considered. Perfection is overrated. It is boring. A life without challenge is not the kind of life that you are prepared to live.

Now, I know that some of you stupid people are going to become obsessed over some goal and thereby make yourselves unhappy most of the time. Do not do that. Unhappiness is correlated very strongly with the number of "must-haves" in your life. Every "must" is a shortcut to unhappiness.

Chapter 15: Truth, why it is overrated, why you do not want it, and why you do not need it

The main problem with truth is that there is only one kind of it. Anybody could say the truth, and it would ideally be using the same words in the same way, which quickly becomes boring. This process does not help the mind to consider alternatives in a way that would be required to fully understand something.

The truth could be said in more stylish ways, but this is a great deal of work. Also, any means of making the truth more stylish will generally make it less true, which is unappealing to those who put great stock in truth.

It is usually more satisfying in many ways to dress up a lie and use it than to dress up the truth. This may seem paradoxical. Consider that when you dress up a lie, it can seem nearer to the truth, and therefore it becomes more appealing. When you dress up the truth, it gains some degree of falsehood and thereby becomes less appealing. This is how the mind works. Lies can be appealing additionally because they tweak cognitive dissonance in potentially appealing ways to gain attention. Truth must keep its absolute quality to retain its full appeal, and absolutes are absolutely restricted.

Stupid people seem to be configured to automatically reject truth as irrelevant or untrustworthy. They may actually run screaming away from truth, but will gladly embrace lies with open arms.

Very few people are able to consciously perceive much truth, except sometimes in potentially life-threatening situations where only the truth is useful. Only then is there enough desperation to make people grudgingly resort to truth. Even after all that, people may not be prepared to perceive the truth, and may even die rather than adapt to an unfamiliar but accurate bit of information.

For many, especially for those who are heavily immersed in entertainment, the truth may be a completely alien concept that they would never wish to grasp. Accurate information may seem distant, boring, unimportant, or disturbing to stupid people, and the reasons for stupid rejection of knowledge are probably as complex as the thinking power of billions of stupid minds.

There is attention to be gained when there are relatively few liars in a society full of honest people, which is reason enough for some opportunists to lie like their lives depended on it. This only works if most people are trying to tell the truth. If everyone is trying to lie, falsehood becomes boring and commonplace for all except the most skilled liars. Being the one honest person in a room of liars typically yields no reward.

Still not convinced that truth can be a bad thing? Consider the person who is always honest. Eventually that person will say something that you do not like. This is sometimes called, "lacking a filter," and is considered to be a social faux pas. People are very happy to not be reminded of inconvenient truths. "But what about useful truths," I hear some of you saying in your keening whiny voices. Nobody likes those truths either, or at least nobody who counts likes them.

Just try telling people true things that they did not know, and make it clear that you consider these things to be truths. Many people will become defensive, because they will feel like they should have known these things already. Many will try to disprove what you told them, through boredom if nothing else. It takes a strong person, or paradoxically a very passive person, to hear an unfamiliar truth in a socially acceptable way.

As an exception to much of the above, stupid people may frequently perceive only one, typically newly understood, truth. Regardless, the stupid habit of going overboard takes over here, and these stupid people will use their one truth like some type of wonder drug to inappropriately try to solve all kinds of problems that are not even tangentially related. I already complained about this above or below this passage, but I must repeat it here because you are stupid.

Chapter 16: Why being good is a bad thing in the bad way

Many feel guilty when near good people, and many celebrate whenever a good person is shown to have done even one bad thing. Good behavior is therefore not as liked as you may think it is. I do not expect this to be immediately accepted by the reader, because it is one of the most paradoxical things in society. Bear with me, and I think you will see the point. Remember this as you go along: consider all the bad people that you know, and chances are that all of them have more nice things than their immediate peers.

When encountering a perceived good person, stupid people are often reminded of their own shortcomings, suspecting that this inconvenient good person may turn them in to the authorities or scold them for not being impossibly good. Stupid people may wish to reap the rewards that come with the praise that good people receive, but any denial of appetites does not sound as fun. Because inner-critics tend to be irate and extreme, any unfavorable comparison with the good person feels bad.

When encountering a so-called "bad" person, often a self-styled rebel or flourishing rulebreaker, stupid people behave according to different rules. Stupid people wish they were like the rulebreakers who are successful.

Successful rulebreakers live exciting lives by breaking only the dumb rules. The inner critic can come into play regarding rebels, but in a different way. It makes stupid people feel inadequate when the rebel shows strength or succeeds at some other primal feat.

This is not to say that all rulebreaking is exciting or liked. Rulebreakers must be savvy to flourish. If they break the wrong rules, they will fail, and fewer people will want to be like them after that.

When good people lapse, they feel guilty and they show it. Guilt teaches others a way to dislike anyone who is showing it. When bad people lapse, they either lapse into goodness momentarily or break the wrong rule. Regardless, they do not feel guilty in a way that seems weak to a stupid person. A skilled bad person only shows this guilt strategically, and not otherwise when others could see it. Guilt felt by a good person is like pain and it shows. Bad people become angry and defensive when feeling guilty, and this can be mistaken as strength or is otherwise relatable.

Nobody wants to be that person who is earnestly feeling the pain of guilt or remorse. Stupid people want to be the one who is fighting against the pain and striking out against accusation. This is true whether anyone is actually accusing or not, because the inner critic will pick up the slack. These patterns should not be too difficult to understand once considered properly. We generally want to be fighters, not victims. We do not want to be misunderstood. We do not want to be the victims of accusations. We do not want to be the victims of our own inner critics.

Once fortresses of stupidity are built around all of this, it grows to the point that one bad thing done by an otherwise saintly person "justifies" a lifetime of bad behavior from a bad person, in the eyes of stupid people. It also "justifies" normal behavior that stupid people feel guilty about for stupid reasons.

A good person is therefore the target of scrutiny from everyone who has done anything bad or feels guilty for any reason. Few understand the motives of a good person. What kind of thing do they want to steal? Which rights of others do they wish to violate? If the answer to both questions is "none," then many people will assume that this allegedly good person is lying or deeply repressed. This is why you will not have enough nice things for as long as you are consistently good.

Nothing is less appealing or less popular than what we should be doing but are not doing. Give someone a "should," and they will give you back a groan. Likewise, rules are deeply unpopular things. Rules are generally not needed to forbid unappealing things, laws concerning donkeys and bathtubs notwithstanding. The only way that a rule or a "should" evokes feeling is if it goes against an appetite.

Not many people go out of their way to tell you that you should not eat leather, for instance, and nobody wants to eat leather. There is no appetite satisfied by doing so. If you irately started telling everyone to stop eating leather however, someone would try it to discover what they were missing.

This is not to say that all existing rules are good. There are some conspicuously bad rules out there, and societies seem to have an effectively infinite capacity for generating more of them. We are all aware of this, which is a very good reason why so many people dislike strict followers of rules. Why be controlled by people who make bad rules?

Rulebreakers are "bad" people that are well-liked because they teach us how to deal with societies that are densely filled with arbitrary rules. Flourishing rulebreakers prove their superiority over those who must suffer under the yoke of an ever-excessive number of useless rules. Flourishing rulebreakers know that some of the best rules are unwritten. A successful rulebreaker succeeds through breaking the right rules and by not breaking the wrong ones.

We are taught about the excitement of flourishing rulebreakers in fiction, the most convincing teacher in existence, because rulebreakers make for exciting stories. This is not to say that every story about a rulebreaker portrays this consistently or well, but many memorable stories strike a chord in this respect.

I am not trying to say that all good behavior is bad or disliked. Saints are mildly liked but follow a rough road.

Unexpected goodness is often appreciated, as long as nobody feels guilty about it and as long as it is not a social faux pas. Unexpected goodness therefore works best in small doses and with low frequency.

Likewise, badness is not always seen as fun. Unexpected badness is at least temporarily disliked, as long as we do not feel mean while condemning it, and as long as it does not happen to us.

I am saying that all the above described patterns, taken together, can explain why society loves forthright villains and disdains apparent heroes who try and fail to be good. This at least slightly favors not trying to be good at all, unless you can pull it off perfectly.

Stupid people believe only in absolutes. They believe in absolute saints and absolute villains. Both are accepted just fine, and both are completely impossible.

Nobody likes failed saints, and nobody will forgive them, because unexpected badness from a saint, even a single lapse, is seen as a betrayal. It suggests that failed saints are frauds or repressed individuals who would be better off living according to their natures.

Many of us adore villains who "lapse" into unexpected good behavior, however. In this case the lapse is taken to show that villains are really only misunderstood and too harshly judged. This makes us feel better about whatever we were stupidly feeling guilty over, because it teaches us a way to dismiss condemnation as misunderstanding.

We all feel misjudged sometimes. We all feel misunderstood sometimes. This is why we can relate to known villains who seem to be trying to be better people. We will therefore forgive a villain who lapses into an accidental good act, in part because it can help us forgive ourselves. Additionally, we would feel bad if we tried to scold a villain who just now did something good.

Nothing comparable exists to help us relate to lapsed good people. Nobody wants to be worse than people expected us to be. We may relate to that in some way, but not in a way that we want to dwell upon.

Many of us want to be rebels, because rebels have said no to something important at some time in their lives. It seems too easy and too boring to blindly follow all rules. Most of us instead want to point to at least one rule and say no. Some of us may be too afraid to do that, but the rebel is not. This combines with the natural fun of naughtiness to be even more fun.

Few of us want to be the opposite, potentially a wishy-washy yes-person. When no other context is supplied, there is no guarantee that non-rebels have ever said no to anything. Since stupid people are doing the thinking here, the bored ones often want to be rebels against all authority, carrying it overboard as stupid people typically do. This is one reason why so many stupid people are against obviously right things for no good reason.

Little exists to reinforce strict rule followers as individuals relative to one another. Either you try to follow all rules, or you do not conceptually fit into this category. Rulebreakers can exist across a larger spectrum that provides far more opportunity for establishing and advertising individuality.

Stupid people believe only in impossible absolutes. You are either all good or all bad in their eyes. Therefore, they will only accept your errors if your errors make you and themselves seem a little better than a real or imagined critic could imply.

There is a mystique that goes along with flourishing rulebreaking. It is a type of personal magnetism, an energy of personality that can be exciting. This effect could fade if it escapes the extremely short memories of stupid people, however, and so you should reinforce this by being occasionally bad in relatable and understandable ways. You can spice things up by occasionally lapsing and doing a good thing by apparent accident.

Do not be a saint, unless you are some unicorn-like smart person that nobody understands anyway. Nobody truly likes saints, except after they are dead. Then, they rip you up and carry your knucklebones about to various different parts of the world, which is probably not exactly what you want.

Chapter 17: Nobody is right all the time, and nobody is wrong all the time

One of the most frequent traits of stupid people is that if they find you being "wrong," then you are forever wrong in their eyes. Likewise, if you are "right" often enough, they will believe that you are always right. I put those words in quotes because stupid people have no idea when a statement is actually right or wrong. They do have some type of instinct used for interpretation, which seems to reference a combination of speaker confidence, immediate reactions from others, some vague interpretations of body language, and primal guesses about the speaker's personality.

If you are caught being wrong, stupid people will assume that everything about you is also associated with your wrongness. Your clothing, hair, skin, facial shape, size, body shape, gender, age, apparent economic background, and every other noticed detail about you will also be considered wrong on this topic as well and as potential causes of the wrongness.

This happens even in the minds of stupid people who are not consciously discriminatory, and it goes beyond frequent focuses of discrimination itself, down to amazingly granular details. This phenomenon may certainly contribute to stereotypes and caricatures that can be intended elements of discrimination, however.

The association of wrongness with finely granular noticed traits may be closely linked to ancient disease-avoidance mechanics in our instinctive behavior. For nearly all of human history, people had no idea how diseases spread, and every detail was potentially suspect. This method of diagnosis has likely become instinctive, and stupid people listen more strongly to their instincts than to reason. For these reasons, I believe that stupid people regard wrongness as something like a mysterious disease. They have no idea why a person is wrong, but they are damn well going to make a wild guess.

Stupid people believe that there must be a correct opinion concerning every topic, no matter how subjective it is, no matter how little we know about it. They believe that we know the best opinion on the topic right now, and that there is no benefit in considering any other possibility. They would prefer zero deliberation, or they want any deliberation to entertain the possibility of correctness for only one opinion.

Stupid people are not open to the idea that all available opinions could be inaccurate. It also does not matter to them how unimportant the topic is, and they will go on aggressive personal crusades until the disfavored opinion is gone. This reveals that stupid people do not necessarily wish to have accurate opinions, but they do want to immediately eliminate all conflict between opinions.

At no point do they believe that there is any benefit in considering alternatives, never mind that humanity has greatly benefited through doing exactly that. Weakness is the worst sin to a stupid person, and indecision is considered to be weak even if it is only fleeting.

It is no surprise to find stupid people trying to eliminate variant opinions, because their world is overwhelming and confusing. Through eliminating things to consider within their insufficient minds, stupid people hope to gain stability that they cannot actually gain. When their world becomes simpler, stupid people make it complicated again by fruitlessly obsessing over pointless thoughts more often to fill the void.

In almost no circumstance will a stupid person test the factual value of any statement. However, they will never entirely abandon guesses about other people's personalities and appearances as criteria for "rightness." In nearly every case, someone who satisfies all the criteria for "rightness" will be considered always right, unless contradicted by someone who satisfies the criteria in a better way. This serves in the place of actual verification because stupid people are not capable of properly verifying a statement, and they may be somehow aware of this.

Stupid people would probably not believe you if you told them how to verify a statement, because such a thing would deeply conflict with their concepts of truth and falsehood. It is probably best to not ask them to verify things, because they are not good at it. Do you ask turtles to fly? I hope not. Then do not ask stupid people to do smart things.

Stupid people do not realize that statements are best evaluated on their own merit, completely independent from who said or wrote the statements. Confidence can be a result of knowing that one is speaking accurately, but stupid people assume that confidence is the cause of accuracy. In case you have not already guessed, this is why every stupid person is easy prey for a con artist.

Likewise, stupid people are highly reliant on agreement from gaggles of other stupid people for verification. If a gaggle of stupid people rejects anything, even obvious things such as the existence of the Moon, then any stupid bystander will agree with the gaggle instead of with any other source. This may even be wise, because gaggles of stupid people can kill you for no good reason.

There are rare circumstances when rightness criteria are not upheld consistently. This invariably leads the stupid person to long-term confusion. This confusion will persist until a perceived right person clears it up. Stupid people will not make any serious attempt to solve the problem on their own, but instead can become increasingly anxious until they break something.

In a few rare cases, stupid people's verification processes can become more complex but will not decrease in strangeness.

If you happen to be right about academic subjects, but fail to satisfy any other rightness criteria, stupid people will assume that you know all useless things but nothing useful. This is an example of guessing about other people's personalities, but it is also a wild attempt at trying to detect an overspecialized stupid person. This attempt will generally fail, such that overspecialized stupid people are considered globally "right," while people with common sense are often considered overspecialized. If these errors in judgement did not happen frequently, stupid people would not be called stupid.

An extension of this occurs if someone disagrees with dogma or with other things that are incorrectly "known" to be true. This is one of the rare situations in which a "right" person can become "wrong." This often leads to death by being drowned, burned, or pummeled with stones, which are all things that you do not want.

Wit is one of the rare forms of self-defense that the unicorn-like intelligent person can have against stupid people. Wit of high complexity can cause stupid people to accept you as globally right. This is why "bullshitting," or saying nonsense with wit, is an excellent way for con artists to claim to know things that they do not know. However, poorly employed wit inspires suspicion. Stupid people want witty uneducated geniuses laughing with them, but they are somehow aware that it is not good for anyone to laugh at them.

Chapter 18: You are stupid because you think in keywords and symbols

Stupid people believe that speaking rapidly is a sign of intelligence. Since nobody understands most of what you say, speaking rapidly will ensure focus on one key word that is supposed to explain the whole sentence, and it will be taken as a sign of intelligence because you are able to speak quickly while planning what you say. This also confuses stupid people who would be otherwise prone to argue or question stupid information, and it gives the speaker a better opportunity to smoothly retract words that turned out to be mistaken. Be aware that this could cause stupid people to think that you are intelligent, which may not be a good thing if they decide to kill you with blunt objects.

The one word that explains the fast talker's sentence can be called a keyword. It works because one word really can carry a whole paragraph or even a book's worth of ideas with it, if it is the right word used in the right way. This works through its association with something that has in the past broken through the concrete around a stupid person's mind. The whole complex idea gets stored, but not exactly as it entered. The keyword is stored intact, however, and can restore the feeling that was associated with the idea.

It is true that not much enters through concrete walls, but not much exits through them either. This makes the keyword potentially necessary for pulling the associated feeling out of a stupid person's mind efficiently, avoiding confusion in communication.

This would all work wonderfully if stupid people did not muck it up.

A famous example of thinking in keywords is the negative connotation associated with the word "chemical." This occurs even though everything has a chemical formula, including what makes up your body, and everything in and on it. Yet, stupid people want to ban dihydrogen monoxide (water) if we call it a chemical. Likewise, you can make someone afraid of light if you rightly point out that light is a form of radiation.

Because people do not understand words, they latch onto a keyword such as "chemical" or "radiation," when far more words are required to tell you what kind of chemical or radiation is good or bad. And yes, I guarantee you that every good object is also composed of chemicals. Good light is a form a radiation. Bad objects are also composed of chemicals, and harmful radiation is still harmful.

Stupid people cannot comprehend these simple statements at all. Words are a struggle for stupid people, and they can handle maybe one at a time, or zero. Their desire to know when to run away screaming far outstrips their desire to understand anything. After all, very little understanding is required to run away screaming, but probably not even an infinite amount of fear would lead to any type of productive understanding.

Thinking in symbols is a more primal form of the lazy habit of thinking in keywords, and we fall back on it at times. That is, once a person becomes too lazy to even think in keywords, symbols are the next easiest thing. Therefore, all the false beliefs that stupid people attach to keywords additionally become attached to all sorts of other objects. I say this because every object in the mind of a stupid person is a symbol. This is why stupid people may completely misunderstand what a drawing on a wall represents, becoming irate for no good reason until somebody stops and tells them how stupid they are.

Extreme reliance on symbols and rehearsed reactions is also why many people are afraid of things that they have only "encountered" in television and movies. The sounds used in such media, while entertaining, become associated with things that never make such sounds. People remember the sounds while running in fear from harmless things, and would swear that these things made the same sounds that were heard in the movies. This is all an illusion in the minds of lazy people who have much more contact with vague subconscious notions, movies, and television, than with reality.

I have probably lost most readers already, you all being stupid, but let us persist because this is more important than you think it is. When a person equalizes arbitrary symbols with real objects in their mind, it inevitably results in many problems. This may be a side-effect of some minds not being properly adapted to the massive amount of metaphors in our lives.

You could view metaphors as lies that point to something, as long as you do not misunderstand this statement and lose your mind. All art, and all stories, are lies. I point this out to explain to you that your world is filled with benign lies, no matter what you do. All societies are built largely on lies, and these benign lies are necessary for what we call humanity.

Even a benign lie is an intelligence test, and stupid people are limited in their ability to overcome such challenges. It should not be surprising to find out that many stupid people cannot handle such a complex system of lies, or that they can turn it inadvertently into something malign instead.

Our lives are filled with abstract references of references, all eventually pointing to a thing that is real in some way, but generally concealing that thing and sometimes failing to distinguish it from others.

Even talk of Bigfoot references something: a myth that can be instructive about people even though Bigfoot does not exist. Talk of the Statue of Liberty references something: an actual statue. Yet, some stupid people will insist that Bigfoot is as real as the Statue of Liberty, for one or more stupid reasons.

These reasons may include a lack of experience with the material world, but more often the biggest reasons include the need to alleviate boredom, distrust of rational information, and excessive trust of intrigue. All these and other reasons are succinctly summed up as "stupidity" in this book, but you should know that already.

Chapter 19: Those stupid false narratives that you like are not true

Stupid people hold large numbers of incorrect beliefs, but some of the worst are false narratives that they tell themselves about themselves and others. These narratives need not be entirely false, but generally are, and are full of lazy conclusions and other ills that arise from the minds of stupid people.

I could have made each type of narrative a different chapter, but false narratives are important enough to get more focused attention than that. You may connect this with the Fortresses of Stupidity or Rat Tunnels that I mentioned earlier. Such phrases are helpful, but I plan to go beyond that here. Woe to you stupid people who were already lost before we got here.

First off, many of those afflictions that you may think you have, many of your diagnosed shortcomings and disorders, things that you are supposedly good or bad at, are lies or exaggerations made up to excuse laziness. This is one of the most powerful forces in the minds of stupid people. Laziness makes the world not go round.

When stupid people do not wish to do something inconvenient, they may suddenly become aware of an affliction that prevents honest people from doing the same thing. Adopting this affliction (but not actually suffering from it), the lazy stupid person gains many things: no longer needing to do the inconvenient thing, and gaining sympathy from other stupid people who would like to care but are too lazy to care only about things that are actually true.

Some stupid people see great benefit from claiming many afflictions, none of them actually present and none diagnosed by a responsible professional. Some stupid friends tolerate this behavior because they cannot be bothered to argue with an extremely lazy person who is only dedicated to not living as an adult. If presented with enough incentive, the "afflicted" stupid person suddenly regains the skill that was supposedly lacked.

It should be obvious by now that adopting false afflictions is a means of living in the womb, which is a favorite pastime of stupid people. This should never be tolerated, but stupid friends tolerate all sorts of terrible things.

Let us continue scolding in an aside. Adopting an affliction that you do not actually have, can be to some degree an honest mistake, especially if disreputable professionals enable such behavior. Regardless, it is disrespectful to those who actual have real health issues. You can be disrespectful if you want, but it is your fault when I yell at you for doing that.

Some of these "afflictions" are made-up shortcomings instead of made-up disease diagnoses. One of my friends is a university graduate in a science field, but she repeatedly told everyone that she could not do statistics. This was the start and usually the failed end of everything that she ever did that involved the calculation of any probability. Many of the rest of you stupid people sympathize with this. Yet, I am telling you that statistics is not inherently more difficult than most of the rest of the things that you do every day, such as driving, socializing, or whatever you do in your job.

There are some other university graduates who are convinced that they cannot drive, for instance. They create narratives after they do something wrong once or a few times, the narrative claiming that they "will never" and "cannot" do something that is really only unfamiliar instead of difficult.

I am not trying to single out university graduates here as especially stupid, by the way, but I mention this to establish that these individuals are competent enough to do other things that require thought. I am establishing that if even university graduates can make themselves fail at simple things, then anybody else can replicate this feat of stupidity. I also raise the possibility that maybe, just maybe, you could do these things easily if you just internally shut up and did them one step at a time, instead of wasting so much effort making yourself feel bad.

These narratives cause many a young student to believe that they can never guess what 60 divided by 12 is. Or if they know that, they may decide that they will never understand x when x = 60 divided by 12.

Your mind is powerful. Yes, even, or especially, a stupid mind is powerful. When fully dedicated to anything, it tends to be effective. When you spend all your mind's energy telling yourself that you cannot do something, you tend to be very convincing. This is also at least comparable to some jerk leaning over your shoulder and constantly screaming that you cannot do something. That would be distracting for most people, and congratulations: that jerk is yourself.

If you took some energy away from that jerk (and that jerk does not deserve such an allotment of energy), and dedicated it to simple problem solving, things would get done. You would be able to calculate probabilities, drive a car, fix your own door, paint, write a book, or do any other simple thing.

In today's world, such a broad range of simple skills would make someone seem like a super-person, but this is because today's world is filled with unnecessary discouragement that arbitrarily and falsely limits people. In other words, we accept too many people's false narratives when they tell us that they cannot do simple things.

We believe naysayers when they wrongly imply that we must start perfect in order to be good at something. You are included among the naysayers that you should not be listening to. I am absolutely sure that you can attain at least basic skill in everything, because basic skills are all simple and tend to require simple capacities. That is: if you can do one of them, you can do them all.

For instance, my friend who "cannot do statistics" had no trouble working with numbers in other ways, such as balancing her personal budget. It was only in an academic setting involving numbers that the Inner Jerk became triggered to yell at her.

Some of the more perceptive among you stupid people may already realize that this whole phenomenon is just a special case of stupidity by thinking in keywords and symbols. Words are symbols, and numbers are symbols too. Her Inner Jerk became triggered by the terminology and symbols of academic statistics.

The key to silencing the Inner Jerk is to deprogram this lazy keyword-oriented thinking, in other words: reversing the brainwashing. Start with the simple things, learn how to do them, then come back a few hours or days later to tackle it again. Tell the Inner Jerk to shut the hell up every time it says anything. Keep doing this until you internalize better habits. By that I mean: do this every day for a while. Internalization happens when you do something over a span of days. Much of it happens while you are sleeping, when your mind sorts out things that had trouble traveling from cognitive thought into rehearsed responses.

Once you are very sure of the simple things and are bored with them, move on to something slightly more complex and stick with it until it is similarly internalized and unforgettable. Eventually the Inner Jerk will shut up and let you do things, because internalization of simple parts of the subject will make it so intriguing to you that the Inner Jerk gets no attention.

It is something of a misnomer to use the word lazy in these cases. The Inner Jerk eats up a great deal of energy, and we are not lazy in subsidizing the efforts of our Inner Jerk. We may believe that our least favorite subject takes up more energy than the Inner Jerk does, but I doubt it. Lazy people can be energetic for short periods of time, but the Inner Jerk works all the time if we encourage it too much.

Note that I do not tell you to practice, because that was tried before and did not work. In your stupid mind, you associate the word "practice" with frustrating hopeless work that you could not do. This was all because something interesting appeared on television when you had planned to practice, but I digress. Instead, I told you how to do this right, and I did not give it a label that you can misuse to wrongly discourage yourself. This is not practice, at least not in the way that you think it is.

In a few cases, you may be better off sleeping more functionally, drinking less, or quitting other addictions to facilitate learning simple things. Bad habits slow you down, but if you live long enough, you can learn any simple thing. In short, stop telling me all about what you supposedly cannot do. I do not want to hear such lies.

Labels can be used to assign stigmas in the minds of those who make or use negative narratives. People who have been found to have a "mental problem," no matter how minor or treatable, are stigmatized in this way. Many a person has persecuted family members with supposed "mental problems" over these supposed failings, none of them understanding a thing about it.

Many a false narrative has been created in the mind of supposedly, but not actually, afflicted people, explaining and justifying ill treatment coming from themselves and others. Again, this just makes it tougher on those who have real problems, because everyone starts assuming that every problem is due to non-rejectable potential causes such as stress. It can be difficult to distinguish stress from most any other affliction, but stress is not everything.

Let me continue ranting about diagnoses that cannot be rejected. You are not using a scientific approach to medicine if you diagnose issues as caused by stress and have not rejected alternatives. If you cannot eliminate the possibility of something, then it is not a real diagnosis at all. And guess what: stress can never be eliminated as a possible cause of any affliction. Everyone has stress. Yet, it is not the cause of every problem. This is part of why the p-word discipline has a bad reputation. It is very a bad thing when done poorly.

Other labels take on different and mostly bogus meanings, all undeniable in the minds of stupid people, based on the simple thoughts associated with them. Social anxiety is seen as insurmountable, permanent and unchangeable in the minds of stupid people, for instance. In reality, it can be trained away through deprogramming and focused effort. Some stupid people reach a comfort zone in perpetuating it, and those stupid people may include yourself, your friends, strangers who are triggered when witnessing your anxiety, or all of the above.

We are highly reluctant to adjust concepts of ourselves and others, because we are stupid and do not wish to stop re-thinking the same stupid thought in our heads for long enough to change our minds on anything. Let us be clear about this: a mistake is a potential teacher, not a sign of an affliction.

Chapter 20: The only things that matter to you are subconscious

It may not be surprising that stupid people let their subconscious do all the important thinking. Unfortunately, the subconscious is miserably stupid too. It is full of fears of imaginary things, fears of impossible things, suspicions of impossible things, and fears of things that are possible but which never happen.

Even if some of the possible feared things did happen, the conscious mind would end up dealing with them while the subconscious is taking a break. The subconscious has a purpose, but it does not help much when it is over-used or does not get enough time to do its job.

Like everything else, the subconscious is not good at doing things that it should not be doing. It is good for eventually figuring out that impossible things are actually impossible, without us having to understand exactly why, for instance. It helps quell irrational fears, because rational thought is highly limited in its capacity to do so.

Try to get some decent sleep so that the subconscious can work through its stupid processes, and try to use your conscious mind for the real up-front thinking. Your conscious mind is stupid too, but two stupid processes happening at once feed into the Stupidity Synergy Principle.

What is the Stupidity Synergy Principle? you might stupidly ask. When more than one stupid person is communicating together, their stupid thoughts build upon each other in a way that is greater than the sum of their stupidities.

There is no such thing as an Intelligence Synergy Principle. This is because stupidity is earnest and trusted, while intelligence is often distrusted or misunderstood. Stupidity gets attention, but intelligence is more frequently ignored. Misunderstood stupidity tends to lead towards more stupidity, while misunderstood intelligence does not lead to more intelligence. Distrust of intelligence works slightly differently in that it can be channeled into useful investigation, but this usually does not happen. All of this explains why having two intelligent people in a room is usually a waste of at least one intelligent person, but two stupid people in a room tend to produce a great and powerful stupidity that goes far beyond expectations.

A stupid subconscious, that is not properly able to do its job, is struggling to keep up at the same time that a stupid conscious mind is misunderstanding the world around it. This results in an unfortunate situation that is similar to having two stupid people in a room together, making a person much more stupid than what would usually be expected.

This causes anxiety, because the subconscious does not get a proper opportunity to figure out that impossible things are impossible, or how things that did not happen have not happened. It does not get a chance to tell you that you are going maybe just a little overboard feeling guilty for something 15 years after everyone else has forgotten about it.

The conscious mind is overloaded by having to deal with such things, since it can only rarely correlate its understanding of things that do not make sense. Also, it already has plenty of work to do with making sure that you do not offend all the other stupid people that you must impress. Having all your unresolved subconscious fears bubble up to your conscious mind, while awake and struggling with daily challenges, just upsets the whole apple cart.

Chapter 21: People are the root of all evil, also the root of all good and of all sorts of other things

Most of the world's problems arise from people, from you and/or others. Most solutions also arise from that same source, but people in general produce far more problems than solutions. People are probably not responsible for a meteor falling on your head, which constitutes one of the few exceptions to the above statements. Barring that, everything that you are worrying about is probably due to some person and can be solved or prevented by some person.

This might be taken to imply that problems are always avoidable or easily solved, which is exactly what I am **not** trying to say. It is good to try to recognize when problems are avoidable or easily solved, but I am sure that you are too stupid for that.

I do not maintain that the concepts of good and evil are useful, because they refer to the stupid idea of all or nothing. Still, they are useful words for motivating stupid people.

Maybe it is not specific enough to say that people are the cause of all this and that and just move on. If you really must have a more specific root of evil, it is most definitely not the love of money. People who love money a great deal do cause harm by desperately snatching it up, withholding it, and acting as if it is the only important thing in the world. However, all the worst qualities of a love of money stem from something else. Also, many of the people who whine about a love of money would probably trample many innocents just to grab a few thousand dollars dropped on the ground.

All of this is better explained as an obsession with being better than others, instead of simply the love of money. I hear a bunch of you already with your all-or-nothing whining, saying that it is all right to want good things. This makes you stupid. Did I not say "obsession?" That is more than simply wanting decent things in life.

Obsession means that you are desperate to be better than those that you know. Desperation to be better than others causes you to be abusive in many ways. It causes tremendous wastefulness because you are afraid to be seen with less-than-perfect things. It causes far too much anxiety and damages lives every day. It can drive huge massacres without a twinge of conscience. Instead of feeling bad about all that, these obsessed, desperate stupid people feel bad when somebody else has something better than they do!

If there is greater harm to society than obsession over being better than others, then I have not seen it. Yet, even this obsession is not always bad. Especially in today's culture, there is little else to motivate people other than the desire to be better than others. Without this, and without an alternative and more functional concept of simply having enough, people become listless and despondent, with lives full of suffering while wallowing in addictions and anxiety. A concept of "enough," would prevent this, but that is too weighty a thought for stupid people to handle. Just as "some" does not exist in the mind of stupid people, this sense of the word "enough" is also absent.

When stupid people use the word "enough" they use it to mean either too much or too little. Stupid people have mistakenly over-adapted to a world that always demands more, by concluding that it is not possible to simply have enough.

I am also not advising you to be satisfied with a bad situation. You should always try to improve yourself, but not in desperation.

The human mind is not well-suited to being satisfied with "enough." This is probably because information about life is always incomplete, and what was enough for some people in the past was not enough for cultures who conquered them and killed them all. Still, I think you can do it. You can live with enough, and you can refuse to give people permission to be desperately greedy. Be strong.

But what about a root of all good? Not much is ever said about that. Possibly you have seen the above statements that I am not convinced that ideological systems have necessary opposites. This is one reason why I did not simply locate the opposite of obsession over being better than others, so that I could put a sign on it saying "good."

In other words, I do not believe that the desire for equality is the cause of much good. No part of life can take true equality into account. There are differences, even if they are situational and genetic. Every time that it has been tried, every system based on equality has been taken over by power-hungry, cruel individuals who were desperate to be better than others. This is not to say that it is impossible to get such things in the future, but we do not have the required understanding that must occur as a stepping stone towards that goal. Trying to have a fully equal society, put into place immediately, would be like giving a computer to a cave man.

Instead, as a society we must resolve the problems that we have today. Progress towards an apparent future utopia will happen along the way. This cannot happen when people are fully dedicated to preventing any possible resolution to any problem.

Consider that one of the few things that cause us to do good things is a boost in what I have called mood health, sometimes called spiritual health.

We feel good when we know that we have benefitted a worthwhile charity, even if opinions differ over the best charities. We do not feel the same kind of good when we benefit a known scam foundation, even if we may profit monetarily. It is not the same feeling and does not promote anything that we call goodness. We feel good in a non-selfish way when we benefit something outside ourselves that we perceive as good. Therefore, to me, the root of good is mood health. You know it when you feel it: a feeling of cleansing and benefit, without guilt and without the idea that you have done harm to something. It makes us feel like we have benefitted something larger or more persistent than the concerns of the moment, even if that something is nature, family members, the poor, our own bodies, or research.

Because mood health is boosted subjectively, I could re-word this by saying that knowledge that you have done good is reinforcement for future good actions. Just about anything could improve mood health in different people, because the flexibility of the human mind is extreme.

You could lie about it and contribute to a scam that gives you more money back than you contributed, but you would still know it and would not feel the same. Even if you build a Fortress of Stupidity around it, you will still know on some level that the fortress hides a lie. This awareness will cause you to feel guilty and you will lash out at innocents. Even if you blame all these feelings on others, you do not gain mood health from any of that.

Chapter 22: Stupidity has nothing to do with demographics

Society stupidly adheres to a remarkably narrow idea of demographic adequacy. In order to be adequate, you must be supposedly a tall white heterosexual male with perfect muscular tone, no blemishes, a good voice, and no health issues at all. Only a small number of people fit into this category, and all other people feel inadequate for not measuring up to such a primitive measure. Note that I say "adequacy" instead of "perfection," because I am trying to teach you a novel concept. And yes, I am aware that you did not understand any of that.

The whole idea behind uplifting only one narrow demographic state is stupid. A range of good and bad people fit the above category, just as for every other category of people. Stupid people exist in every category, as do smart people. My apologies to all the semi-mythical smart people who receive unwanted attention because of what I just said.

There is not really any visible trait that will tell you if a person is acceptable or not. Despite this, nearly every stupid person across the world believes, either overtly or by unwitting agreement, that they can tell if you are acceptable according to whether you have one easily noticed trait or another.

Stupid people who feel bad about themselves because they are not a "tall white heterosexual male with perfect muscular tone, no blemishes, a good voice, and no health issues at all" fall into the category of those who accept this stupid idea by unwitting agreement. You should not have cognitive dissonance about this.

There is an underlying tendency for stupid people to accept or try to reconcile things said by other stupid people, even when those stupid things are obviously wrong. It would be less stupid to bring the idea up into conscious thought and reject it, but stupid people do not like to think. They especially do not want to think when it gets in the way of an exciting conflict. More on that in the next chapter.

Instead of simply thinking, stupid people try to stupidly solve this by obsessing over irrelevant differences. Calling constant attention to differences merely perpetuates exaggerated notions of those differences. Problems become resolved when people realize that demographic differences are irrelevant. Problems do not get resolved when people are screaming constantly about differences.

This is not to say that it is wise to completely ignore age and genetics. When people get older, they need to be responsible enough to get checked for health problems at the right times. They are not absolved of this responsibility by accepting the accurate conclusion that age is not a damning trait. If you have a genetic predisposition to a disease, you are not cured by accepting the accurate conclusion that genetic traits are not damning.

Like any other obsession that stupid people use to waste their minds, constant obsession over demographics will distract you from important things. The one and only person whose mind you can truly change and need to change over this is you. If you fully understand your position, you can and will convince others through leading by example. You sure enough will not change minds by simply yelling louder or more often than others do.

Discrimination is a very lazy practice, because it focuses upon superficial details. Let me be very clear on this: if you are angry with someone, or afraid of someone, or dislike someone, and you believe that some demographic trait is a factor in this, then you are contributing to the problem. It is that simple.

Do not give anyone permission to hate others. Revoke that permission every time you find someone who believes that they have it. Ignoring it will not solve it. Nobody is born with beliefs concerning exactly who to hate. Instead, people hate in ways that they have learned.

Chapter 23: All your tastes, likes, and dislikes are stupid

This world is full of stupid people who will become offended if you like, dislike, or use something that they do not like, dislike, or use. This highlights the tendency of stupid people to increase the complexity of their world until they stop understanding anything. It equalizes petty topics with vastly more important topics in the minds of stupid people, which is very unfortunate. Still, there is a point and a reason for all of this.

When we obsess over trivial things, we are exercising our abilities to think, compare, and communicate. It is too bad that stupid people thereby indicate that they need to exercise these skills far more in order to become good at them, but that is the way of things.

As an expert will tell you, even a tremendous amount of physical exercise will do harm if you exercise in the wrong ways. While it would normally be fine for stupid people to exercise their thinking skills by processing trivial conflicts, they do this exercise in the wrong ways and end up with skills that perpetuate conflict instead of resolving it.

Do not misunderstand: conflict is not always bad. It draws attention to disagreement, which is required to move discussion forward. Disagreement itself is also not bad, and complete agreement is impossible.

Through exploring disagreement, we can develop new ideas instead of simply repeating the same accepted ideas to ourselves in a form of stasis. If a disagreement is dropped without gaining enough attention, it ends up being a complete waste of time.

As in many other cases, stupid people overuse conflict by trying to keep it going indefinitely. It excites them and gets their heart rate going. Many of these stupid people do little else in their lives. Perpetual conflict may be their only known way of reliably becoming excited. They would be greatly disappointed if their source of excitement disappeared through being resolved. This is why stupid people spend great effort avoiding resolution instead of seeking it.

Stupid people tend to do so many things disastrously, and they have discovered ways to cause disaster in this case as well. It is not necessarily bad to have limited but perpetual conflict over trivial issues. It is bad to enforce perpetual conflict over important issues that require a resolution before we can have some nice things. If people go far out of their way to avoid a solution to a problem, they are indicating that either they consider something else to be the real issue, or they consider the possibility of boredom to be a much greater problem.

All of this can result in a society where resolution is an alien concept. This may keep a bunch of otherwise bored individuals excited, but it also prevents people from gaining some very useful skills that could help them in a potential adulthood that they may never truly have. Nobody wants an employee who is simply going to argue all day without accepting a solution to anything. Nobody wants to deal with people who are desperately afraid of letting you be right about something in a way that they did not anticipate. There is a word for those who desperately want to be excited and entertained at all times, no matter the cost: childish.

If you want to find some way to express preference in a constructive way, you can do something friendly and non-dismissive, such as constructively socializing with them and sharing your nice things. Even people that you do not like will learn something good, if they value you as a person. In this process I doubt that you will find a constructive way to prove the unacceptability of dangling prepositions while doing this, and that is certainly no great loss.

It may take a while to convince someone in this way, but you will never convince anyone of anything if you instead indicate that you find them distasteful. People who are considered to be distasteful are always guaranteed to be on the outside, and therefore they have nothing to gain by adopting your opinion. Given that they do not find themselves distasteful, they are likely to determine that your other opinions are just as wrong as your distaste.

Maybe you have not caught on to it yet, but I am telling you that simply forcing an unwanted opinion upon someone is rude and is not to be tolerated. If you do not have nice things to share, then you should probably shut up about your preferences. However, if you do have nice things, you can validly lead by example.

Those who wish to spend all their time arguing stupidly on social media about stupid likes and dislikes can skip this. Everybody knows that you are too bored and stupid to do anything aside from participation in trends. Yes, I told you this only at this late stage just to annoy you. Yes, I know that you like being annoyed.

Please note that I am not recommending that you actually try to fix important things. Stupid people who cannot even properly discuss trivialities have no business bungling important matters. Leave that to people who are not incredibly stupid. This means that you should largely be silent. Seriously, convincing reasonable people of trivialities is easy, and only an intensely stupid person could foul it up.

In a few situations, you can try to constructively guide stupid people by giving them feedback when they are open to it, such as when they have problems that need solving. If your favorite trivial topic cannot solve a problem that matters to them and does not positively affect their quality of life, then you should not share it. If you cannot say it in a way that is convincing, you should shut up and learn how to be convincing.

Stupid people are always overwhelmed by their problems. Chances are that sharing your trivial preferences badly would be the one last thing that was needed before they snap and break things.

Chapter 24: You are stupid because you are not properly stimulated

Many stupid educators (more properly termed anti-educators) do not understand the role of stimulus in education. This is generally taken to frightful extremes, where a topic is taught in boring ways, using boring wording and visuals, in a lifeless and boring room, by bored people who wish that they were doing something else.

Seriously, it does not really take ten years to learn how to solve for x when x equals 8 divided by 2, except that people get bored and only learn that they do not want to know this. It therefore should not be surprising that many do not learn much of anything during their education, except how to properly make a spitball or do drugs on campus without being caught. After all, the latter two topics are "exciting" in part because they are not included among lifelessly presented materials.

Many of those who persist in learning, despite the lack of a stimulating environment, are also stupid people who realize that their only hope in advancement is to paradoxically avoid competition with those who are ignoring education. Many who avoid education in favor of things that are more immediately interesting and more effectively presented, are doing things that are exciting enough to share with others.

Focusing on fun things has many subtle benefits later in life, such as gaining personal contacts and learning the most from available role models. Those who avoid education are also far more likely to gain social skills that will aid them in an adult life that many never truly have.

This is not to say that either the exciting or the boring route leads reliably to a well-rounded individual. Instead, we end up mainly with specialists who sided with either education and boredom, or with intellectual stasis and social excitement. This creates an unnecessary false dichotomy that exists only in the minds of stupid people. Smart people realize that you can have both a good education and good social skills, without paralyzing boredom and without yielding life to addictions.

Those among us who understand our own capabilities are well-advised to wager that we will overcome reasonable challenges. We will be able to take well-traveled, more stimulating, more challenging routes and succeed. Those stupid people who have a low estimation of their skills in anything, regardless of whether it is academic, athletic, or social, are probably underestimating themselves. Stupid people who unjustly condemn themselves will have so much mental static that they will be less successful even at things that they have chosen as a specialty.

But I digress. I went on the previous rant because I wanted to say that a lack of stimulation is a major problem in many people's lives during education. It simply gets education off on the wrong foot.

At early ages, many may not be able to consciously figure out soon enough why they are not learning simple things (such as mathematics). Once we become adults however, we have less of an excuse for this, and we should not perpetuate the problem by making everything more boring than it has a right to be.

Liven up the place and the process a little, so that people will be happy and stimulated enough to be interested in what you are saying! Taking control of your surroundings as an adult can break the cycle that you inherited from other stupid people who reinforced a miserable concept of education. Make your life more stimulating in a healthy way, and it will improve. Everything that you need to do can be done in a way that maximizes what you gain from it. You can have nice things, if you decide to not be stupid and lazy, and if you decide to avoid the inaccurately pessimistic assessments of your stupid predecessors.

Consider that in order to fully understand something, you must be able to understand why alternatives are rejected. Education rarely highlights this. Topics are not interesting when everything agrees, because we then find it difficult to imagine anything different.

Topics are more interesting when some sources or indications disagree. At that stage, meaningful tests can be done. When something confirms what you already believe, you may not learn much. When it conflicts with what you believe, you can learn a great deal. We do not learn much when something operates as expected. We can learn more when something defies expectations.

Consider further that conflict is the most exciting thing in most people's lives, but education tends to avoid much mention of the extreme importance of conflicting opinions in the development of all the nice things that we have. Why not try teaching with conflict? People will remember things better. It will certainly take more work, but you should consider eliminating needless things from the educational process in order to make it operate more smoothly. Instead of graduating a crowd of anxiety-ridden or bored, drug-addicted, unskilled individuals, you could be graduating a crowd of people who can cope with the world outside of the school building.

Finally, hope and a vision for advancement are required for anyone to care about learning. Lasting improvement occurs when you the increase awareness of opportunities for those who previously had little hope. You are wasting people's time if you teach them things that they do not need. Most of education consists of things that they do need, and therefore, you lie to them when you imply that such things are purely academic and therefore trivial in everyday life. In today's world, our everyday lives rely upon a vast number of facts that seemed boring and useless during most people's educations. As life increasingly welcomes new technology, we run out of excuses for making education boring.

Chapter 25: You are stupid because you trust bad resources

Stupid people implicitly trust scam authorities and resources that appeal to laziness or stupidity. The Internet is full of such things. Lonely and bored friends and relatives, who are otherwise too afraid or too lazy to contact you, spam social media sites and trust everything in them implicitly. These people only do this because they "know" that you like this site and misplace just as much trust in it as they do.

This is why your second cousin (twice removed) is spamming annoying political content to you on a site that you once used for flirting and socializing with people that you are jealous of. These sites may ultimately prove to be a bad idea because they make large sums of money selling your personal information. Some stupid people are now aware of this, but nothing slows these sites down.

This phenomenon is an extension of an old one that has become more visible due to new technology, with older implicitly trusted social scams being replaced by newer ones that are more efficient. Social media have harnessed laziness and social anxiety, thereby gaining billions of dollars because nothing is more frequent than dysfunction.

For some reason (stupidity), once people start misplacing trust, they take it to absurd extremes. This is ultimately how someone across the world, who may not even be able to speak your language, ends up with a solid understanding of exactly how stupid you are, and can then send more or less targeted advertisements to you to capitalize from it.

When you approved of some stupid statement posted by an automated system a few months or years ago, that system recorded that you are a gullible person who believes lies. This information was recorded and is now being used to spam you with more lies that may be tuned to become increasingly appealing to you.

Social media canvassing, and ultimately the fundamental design of the most important sites, arises from a jaded assumption that you are stupid and lazy, and that you are unlikely to learn a damn thing anytime soon. Sound familiar? This is similar to how con artists do the same thing on a personal level. This book also assumes such things, but I am telling you that I am assuming this up front, and therefore you do not place blind trust here. The websites and con artists do not tell you this, and therefore you stupidly trust them with all sorts of personal information.

I do not wish to restrict this phenomenon to social media, however. People trust all sorts of bad things that should never be trusted, because they strike an emotional chord in an otherwise boring time in people's lives. Because we suddenly transition into feeling good at a particular moment, we project that good feeling sloppily all over everything associated with it.

In similar ways, even ancient con artists were able to convince others that they are offering a special deal to only one particular person, when it was really a misleading scam offered to many people across a large area. Before the Internet existed to connect distant relatives, it was desired praise, long-awaited understanding, an entertaining voice, or good looks that served to create the good feelings. This is, therefore, a long-reinforced part of human nature. This all becomes more frustrating when stupid victims decide to reside entirely within the womb on such matters, only listening to those who are manipulating them. Such are the extremes that stupid people can pursue to avoid boredom, when it would be far better to simply find a good hobby and socialize in face-to-face interactions.

If you want to live in a world where most of us behave sensibly and wisely, it is a very good idea to be that social link that keeps some acquaintances from falling into the grasp of con artists.

Do not lazily criticize your loved ones, and do not dismiss them by trying to simplify them or otherwise misunderstand them. Try to speak in a way that helps people feel better (within reason), and try to maintain surroundings in a state that helps everyone feel better. Sometimes this means becoming angry when you must, but it always means behaving according to common sense. Stupid people poorly understand important people in their lives, take them for granted, and make little effort to consistently improve anyone's mood (even their own). Stupid people believe that manipulators all have horns and a pointy tail, never believing that bad influences can be attractive or convenient. This is why you cannot have nice things.

Chapter 26: You are stupid because your body is deprived of necessary resources

Poor maintenance of health is a greatly underappreciated cause of stupidity, but I saved it for late in the book because there is usually some cognitive element as well. Consider that it is possible to create an upward spiral in life, and that it is possible to escape a downward spiral. Exercise, nutrients, sleep, and generally taking care of yourself, could be exactly what you needed to start processes that eventually yield nice things for you. They should not be delayed until you finally get your cognitive issues sorted out. They can be easily among the best steps that you take to potentially stop being so stupid, because they are steps so easily taken.

While cognitive hindrance has great power over rationality and mood, the body's condition strongly influences these as well. In today's world, many nutrient deficiencies result from bad habits such as alcoholism, which can prevent uptake of B vitamins. Vitamin D deficiency can result from rarely going outside or from deficiency in uptake.

Proper thought requires an appropriate daily dose of water and nutrients, because your body can go into survival mode without them. Survival mode cares little about rationality or other troublesome things that bother you in times of emergency. It generally comes into play once your rational mind has failed you.

Proper sleep is an incredibly important requirement for a functional life, and is probably the most underestimated factor. It seems more or less logical, especially to stupid people, to conclude that they can get so much more done if only they did not sleep for 8 hours every day. These stupid people are very

123

likely to wreck their lives by trying to sleep 4 hours or by doing some other stupid thing, always to their own detriment.

Others do not even have the option to get enough sleep, with other stupid people keeping them awake constantly. Sleep is among the most vulnerable things in our lives, because we cannot always afford access to decent sleeping conditions. If you get some money ahead, however, one of the first things that you should do to improve your life is to get a good bed. Poor sleep can very easily create a feedback loop that can become very destructive and difficult to escape. Get good sleep, and be surprised by how much more positive your life will seem.

Some stupid people are genetically hardy, and are strongly resistant to the health issues caused by excessive alcohol. This may make things tough on their drinking buddies, who may not have similarly hardy bodies. Not immediately facing many of the challenges that others face, or not noticing them, hardy stupid people misunderstand much of life. Numerous stupid people believe that they are hardy when they are not, because everyone wants to be one of those strong people who resists anything. Such stupid people seem to think that they can make their cells invulnerable by simply ignoring any possibility of weakness. The body does not work like that. Yet more stupid people make the opposite mistake and act far weaker than they really are, but you knew that I was going to say that.

Many stupid people believe that alcohol is a stimulant, instead of what it really is: a depressant. Alcohol can seem like a stimulant to those who repress themselves, or to those who busily fill their heads with useless thoughts. Once the mind is slowed down to the point that it cannot torture itself as much, a stupid person can feel stimulated because of a clearer mind. However, people who already have a predisposition to melancholy can have this condition exacerbated by alcohol, eventually resulting in tragedy.

Other stupid people deprive themselves of necessary nutrients by failing to ingest a balanced diet. They may also eat too much food that contains unhealthy substances. This includes, but is not limited to, high-sugar, low nutrient foods. Many stupid people eat unhealthy food because some other stupid person told them that it was fine. It is not uncommon for bad health-food websites to contain articles recommending highly inadvisable foods.

Some stupid people are unhappy in part because they do not exercise. Humans did not get this far by sitting around on the couch throughout history, and our bodies are generally not well-suited to such treatment. You do not need to become Charles Atlas, but you do need at least some cardiovascular workouts.

Chapter 27: You are stupid because you do not live in the moment

"Live in the moment" is some of the best advice ever given, but stupid people refuse to follow it. Instead, they fill their days building Fortresses of Stupidity, uselessly re-living past events, and otherwise inefficiently increasing the complexity of their thoughts until they have nothing to spare for perceiving the moment as it happens.

Training ourselves to live in the moment can involve a process of deprogramming. This involves a sad separation from much-cherished self-torturing thoughts that are kept and maintained like favorite toys. Some of these thoughts may have been rapidly repeated millions of times over decades in the mind of a stupid person.

During this deprogramming, Fortresses of Stupidity are torn down, and treasured traumatic past events are forgotten. Stupid people may be unwilling to do this, which is entirely up to them. Not all of us can walk without help, and not every stupid person is able to face the world without relying on stupid thoughts to hide reality from them.

Many stupid people have no idea what life would be like if they were not torturing themselves every single day. Do you really think that such people will gladly turn away from their favorite pastime just because you tell them that there is a better way to live?

The good news in this is that you can probably live in the moment without accepting truth. This requires learning how to simply clear your mind until the moment forces its way into your awareness. A dangerous predator would immediately cause you to live in the moment, because instincts would force this to happen. The ability to make our minds similarly focus on other things exists.

You may believe that stupid people would find it easy to empty their minds, but this is actually exactly the opposite of what a stupid mind is like. Instead of being empty, a stupid mind is running at maximum power, constantly refreshing nonsense, reliving bad memories, re-experiencing recriminations, and reliving other stupid thoughts that do not get resolved. A mind living in the moment is tormented by none of those things, freeing you to achieve what your skills permit.

It would make sense to imagine that everyone would want this, but the human mind is an amazingly convoluted thing. People who have spent enough time on their Rat Tunnels can find reasons to underachieve and self-sabotage. If you really want to fail, I will not stop you, but I suspect that you have moments when you wish that you were succeeding instead.

Chapter 28: You are unhappy because you are stupid

This will be a hard-learned lesson, because your entire world is filled with messages telling you that you will be happier if you have a new car, new house, happier children with the newest toys, and clothing detergent in pods that you should not be eating. None of this will make you consistently happier, and people quickly become listless and bored until they get a slightly better car, house, etc. than those owned by their acquaintances. Once they have the best possible cars, houses, toys, and detergent pods, they become listless and bored once again but without hope of a remedy. Therefore, happiness is only poorly related to the quality of things that you have.

One could say that unhappiness stems from one cause or another, such as inequality for instance. Yet, inequality is guaranteed for humans and all other life forms because of the ways that genetics and chance events work. Someone will always be better, richer, or more liked by others, at least situationally, and therefore inequality will be a glaring flaw in all existence, no matter what we do.

There have been happy people in the past (or in the present but hiding away from stupid people like you) who had far less stuff than their acquaintances had. There have been happy people in the past who were louse-infested, who had no car or horse, who had to work all day for some corrupt loser. They did not even have detergent pods. What if the cause of unhappiness (and the cause of happiness) is a lack of discipline within your own mind?

We have made it to today's human condition in part because we are difficult to satisfy. We always want things that we do not have, but this requires that we be aware of these things.

Many stupid people who lived centuries ago "could only be happy" if they had some trinket that we would likely find unacceptable today. If they had been aware of the comforts that we have now, and associated such things with elements of happiness, they would have wanted today's comforts instead of a bunch of lumpy beads or a bigger codpiece.

They only wanted such things because impressive people had and enjoyed those things. This same pattern occurs across places with varying living conditions today as well. Awareness of the apparently proven value of desirable things could therefore be called a necessary component of both happiness and unhappiness, but it is not the only necessary component.

Self-control must also be a component of happiness, but self-control is also far more complex than stupid people believe it to be. Most associate self-control only with a supposed avoidance of fun, but they exhibit extreme self-control when they believe that it can lead to what they want.

Our minds make complex wagers every day. These wagers occur regardless of our alleged mathematics skills. We precisely and quickly weigh risks and rewards that matter to us. We do not usually leave such things to our conscious minds, which are terribly inadequate. We may let our conscious minds have the lesser job of justifying our decisions to itself and others, but many of us do not even let it do that.

There is variation in our ability to make these wagers, and this plays a large role in what shapes humanity today. You are mostly not aware of this variation, and therefore it works in ways that differ from how we can self-sabotage or self-aid our own math skills, for instance. We do not pay as much attention to variation in our ability to make the above-mentioned wagers, and so we spend more effort observing how others (not ourselves) are somewhat better or worse at them.

Stupid people can fail at both important and unimportant things, and there is variation in the types of stupid people who fail at one or both of these things, but awareness is a requirement for them to build a Fortress of Stupidity around it.

Our conscious minds, which are properly given a number of relatively unimportant jobs, become bored and tend to behave in a cat-like way (this is true even for dog-people). We demand increasingly good things until we are denied, and then we momentarily reduce our demands. These same patterns occur while trying to gain attention from others, which hogs up nearly all of our mental effort, conscious and unconscious.

Attention is a powerful force in our lives. It indicates when another is interested in you and may intentionally interact with you, in either a good or bad way. The ability to notice and interpret attention is deeply ingrained in us, and the processing of attention works very rapidly. Even relatively oblivious individuals rapidly perceive subtle cues indicating when attention is being granted to them. Attention works on such a deep and immediate level for us that it is one of the most important ways of gaining happiness, but it does not work consistently.

We do not always want attention from just any random person, but we prize it from those who have reactions and mannerisms that inspire us to be happy. Attention in high doses from the same person can eventually become mundane, however, no matter how happy they made us in the past. Yet in cat-like ways, we welcome attention from these people again after a period of being ignored. It is therefore a bad idea to give people everything that they want, or to obey all their wishes, or to give them too much attention. Your attention is valuable, but others only realize this if you acknowledge its limited supply.

The power of attention can be highly destructive. We generally become unhappy when we get even the slightest inkling that someone may dislike us. Attention contains the hints that we use for this, and much of our mental activity is devoted to perceiving and processing the attention that we get from others.

Dismissal is a deeply disliked form of negative attention, because it suggests that we did not do the right things to gain positive attention from an individual. Intense negative attention is in a way more rewarding than dismissal, because of the greater effort that it requires. Negative attention can be a form of social negotiation, while dismissal can be a refusal to negotiate at all.

Some stupid people perceive the value of attention as a currency, becoming attention hogs that are seemingly addicted to any sort of attention whether approving or disapproving. This sort of thing becomes obvious even to stupid people after a while, and eventually some may find a way to shut it down by granting types of disapproving attention that even hogs do not like.

Agreement works somewhat differently. Stupid people will not expect your decisions, nor your agreement with their own decisions, to make any sense. After all, stupid people routinely do not make sense and do not generally understand why they should.

Regardless, agreement is valuable currency to stupid people, and they will not appreciate you if you agree with them all of the time, even when they happen to accidentally say accurate things several times in a row. This is the cause of many bad decisions in important matters, where people dispute obvious things just to let everyone know that they are not bootlickers.

Because of stupid absolutist error of believing that individuals are always right or wrong, some powerful people become agreement hogs. These hogs will not allow some less powerful people to be right, even when obviously right, because agreement is such valuable currency that it cannot be left to simply fall into the hands of a peon. This may leave a powerful person no other option than to choose a woefully inaccurate viewpoint and demand agreement on it, which is generally granted no matter how wrong the point, because personal power is far more important to stupid people than is accuracy. This is another reason why you cannot have nice things.

Because we are cat-like (also stupid), we interject negative interactions sporadically into our daily lives. This serves to keep our lives from being boring. Unfortunately, others are seldom in need of conflict at the same times that we are. This generates momentary unhappiness when people needed attention and positive interactions but received rejection and dismissal.

Everyone is equal in value, and so attention from someone else could be just as good or better, if we were only not too stupid to understand this. Also, stupid people often approach interactions lazily, and so they forget how they may have slighted someone else. We do not forget when someone else has slighted us, however.

A reasonably functional method for properly spending valuable social currency, and one which is conducive to happiness, is to react in the short run in ways that make us remembered in a good way.

It is conducive to success to stick in a person's mind, because social currency cannot be spent on stupid people that we have forgotten. Not everyone has the energy to do this, because we spend a great deal of energy obsessing over irrelevant problems that never get resolved. The ability to momentarily break out of the reverie, becoming thereby freed up to spend real social currency on others, is one quickly perceived sign that someone finds us to be important.

Everything that makes you happy also activates one or more dampened feedback loops that will generate some dose of unhappiness in the future, simply because of the way that neurotransmitters and similar substances work in our bodies. This is probably for a good reason, because people who were happy and satisfied all the time probably would have died more readily to various challenges in past eras.

In other words, momentary times of unhappiness (also unfortunate events and unsatisfied desires) drive us to greater achievement, and they drive us to do what is necessary to perpetuate the things that make us who we are. A reality of pure comfort is not a motivating situation.

A book about stupidity cannot be complete without mentioning people who receive too much attention. Because attention is arguably the most valuable currency of all, those who receive too much of it tend to overestimate themselves. In other words, they start to believe that their shit does not stink.

Some of these stupid people probably do have at least one decent skill, but the human mind is powerful enough to overestimate anything. They start to believe that every stupid thought they have is a valuable thing that must be shared, and they may even write a vanity book like this one. They can start to believe that others' worth is only measured by how rewarding the attention feels and how frequently it is given, and they may stop truly evaluating their own opinions. This miserable situation usually leads to grief of one sort or another, especially if received attention decreases and they start wondering why.

Chapter 29: Trolling is controlling

Stupid people are easily triggered. They think in keywords, have many prejudices, and infinitely repeat simple but annoying thoughts in their heads until they drive themselves mad. Stupid people have dozens of rehearsed reactions ready and waiting for someone to say or do the wrong thing. Because of this, millions of bored stupid people can be endlessly trolled nowadays on the Internet, and millions of others spend their days enjoying the sight of this. One of these roles requires serious effort.

The Internet troll must learn keyword triggers and the proper attitude to never admit defeat. Denying defeat by lying and changing the definitions of words is one way to do this. In other words, they use the same old tactics that manipulators have always used. There is generally only a small reward but no punishment for this. Trolls control the scope of your thinking by directing it into small boxes, and they distract attention away from the exits of these conceptual boxes.

Trolled people are not innocents in all this, nor is the unparticipating audience. The troll and the trolled are both starved for attention. You may have guessed it already: trolling and being trolled are simply part of a game that distributes attention. Instead of swindling you out of your money, trolls swindle you out of your time and attention. This reveals a few potentially overlooked needs in human life. We need occasional conflict, for instance, even if stupid people overdo it.

Being trolled lends apparent legitimacy to the trolling effort, because it plays into the controller's desired setting and wastes valuable attention on someone who was likely starved for it. When being trolled, stupid people encourage exactly what they do not like, through rewarding it with the most valuable resource in the world: attention.

No matter how inaccurate a troll's statement, it suddenly gains at least equal footing with whatever the trolled person says. This is why so many bad ideas find new life on the Internet. The legitimacy of your point is damaged when you are trolled, because it is difficult to continue speaking with conviction when the other side refuses to accept anything that you say. This is not to be underestimated as a driving force in society. Trolling can be successful even when the troll is inarticulate, but being trolled is an easy way to destroy any valid viewpoint no matter how well you phrase it.

There are many other methods used in effective trolling, and most belong in a different book entirely. I will mention one more method because it serves as an example of how trolls often work much harder than the trolled: if you make a false accusation that assumes other false accusations to be true, stupid people are much more likely to accept the assumed accusations as true even when they reject the first one. This only works on immensely stupid and lazy individuals, but guess how numerous such people are.

You can easily eliminate trolls from your life, but you probably will not. Trolling follows well-understood and simple rules of social interaction. Face-to-face interactions are less convenient and less predictable. It is easy to turn a troll into a modular part of your life with controlled and limited scope. In face-to-face interactions, we must deal with all the complexities of a real human. Never mind that the troll is real too. Trolls and the trolled mutually agree to not acknowledge that.

Chapter 30: Emotions shape the thoughts of stupid people

Life is confusing for stupid people. They expect dramatic things when the world is mostly mundane. They expect everything to be at extremes, and they expect everyone to be hiding their real motives. This causes stupid people to be constantly at odds with a world that cares nothing about our silly misunderstood concepts.

Cognitive crutches such as absolute categories and absolute extremes, so important to stupid people, do not actually exist in reality. This causes no end of consternation for those who misunderstand both reality and communication. I do not expect you to understand how this leads to stupid misprocessing of emotions, but it may make more sense as I continue.

Nobody cares much about what you do. They only care about how you make them feel. I cannot claim complete credit for this statement. Maya Angelou said something very similar to this before I did. I am jealous over that, even though she and I are saying slightly but importantly different things.

I am saying that people do not care what you do, because many will gladly reward and support a truly horrible person who makes them feel good. This is not necessarily bad, but it reveals much where emotions are concerned. In short, it helps indicate that people are creatures of appetite more than anything else.

All emotions can be called addictive, although they are better described as habit-forming. And yes, I mean all emotions. They deepen to become moods, which further deepen to shape personalities. We are what we remember and focus upon. Self-condemners will remember the times that they fell short. Narcissists will remember times that they succeeded. Other personalities will remember different things fitting their beliefs about themselves.

All types will lie to themselves, creating or exaggerating memories to confirm what they wanted to think. Perceptions of the present and projections of the future are shaped fallaciously in these same ways. Our memories are highly selective. We mainly remember our own, grossly oversimplified, unique version of the most impactful few seconds of an event, ignoring important circumstances that shaped the event itself.

Before we go much further, I need to clarify: so-called negative emotions are not always bad. Every emotion has a role in a normal life, even anger, even hate. They become problems when stupid people misuse them or when other stupid people react inappropriately to them.

Positive emotions indicate that a perceived need has been met. Negative emotions indicate that a perceived need has not been met.

Anger helps us to communicate our needs skillfully enough to be heard. Becoming angry, in appropriate ways and over appropriate concerns, is sometimes among the best things that you can ever do. People only really know you when you put forth a real emotional response delivered with authentic feeling that may need to be intense and abrupt. Anger can cut through cognitive dissonance to express sincerity, where stupid people may be otherwise hopelessly confused while trying to understand what you want. Remember that stupid people see the world through broken lenses. They expect everyone to be as dysfunctional as they are, and cannot imagine that a functional person could possibly exist. Anger can provide just that right amount of apparent dysfunction to put stupid people on the right track in interpreting what you say and do.

Fear of shame and humiliation prevents many misdeeds that laws do not prevent, although these emotions are very frequently overused by stupid people. I have hesitated to mention a good use for these emotions at all, for fear that stupid people will overuse them. This is because many stupid people misuse or misinterpret excitement, converting it through a negative mindset into guilt or shame over nothing. This is a form of negativity-worship, a favorite pastime of the stupid.

Hate indicates that we consider someone or something to be a consistent reason why our needs have not been met. Let me interject here and say that stupid people wrongly believe that negative emotions are always valid and honest, when this is very much not the case. Many negative emotions are expressed by individuals who are immature or lazy, and such individuals can greatly overestimate or overcommunicate their own perceived needs. This phenomenon happens so frequently that it can be a form of manipulation: many stupid people never catch on when an expressed negative emotion is simply a lie or a selfish and childish whine. They do not catch on when negative emotions are simply wrong. This can go on for years, with the overly needy stupid person consistently pushing around those who do not see that they are being mistreated. Do you believe that an overly needy person will stop being overly needy? This will not easily happen when there is no perceived need. The only way out of this is to stop coddling the overly needy and require them to act like adults.

Many stupid people wish to be negative but do not wish to be too confrontational or too honest about it. This wish becomes expressed as cynicism. Other stupid people have no idea what they are doing, but are cynical because they feel helpless. Some stupid people spend whole days being cynical, in part because it helps them feel smarter. After all, if you can reject everything around you, it can mean that there is no way to be a greater failure than your surroundings. This does not happen in a vacuum, and it is not harmless.

Cynicism may well be one of the most harmful things in some societies, because it destroys the motivations of yourself and others. It frequently does so without reference to anything that is actually true, but the cynicism itself can escape any healthy amount of scrutiny. Even when stupid people know that a cynical statement is false, they usually shrug and go along with it because they believe that any number of other negative things make the statement essentially true.

Cynics tend to be disappointed idealists, flipping from one extreme to another, and so their cynicism can be redirected by giving them something idealistic to do that will be harmless when they fail at it.

Positive emotions can be misused as easily as negative ones, but we are quicker to recognize this. Nearly every misuse of a positive emotion can be counted as a social faux pas, while we spend more effort trying to understand negative emotions as clumsy attempts to communicate needs.

In yet another case of the apparent backwardness of stupid people in society, we quickly shame anyone who is too positive, but we may strongly reward those who are too negative. This too has a reason, even if stupid people misuse it: negative feedback can spur us on to become better at what we do.

Without perceived need there is no lasting growth. Even cynicism, a frequent motivation destroyer, can actually motivate when present in small and controlled doses. Society perceives all of this on some level. This is why being excessively nice can be one of the worst things that you can do. I am not telling you to avoid being nice. I am telling you to avoid letting niceness prevent appropriateness.

This is not to say that you should give negative input all the time to supposedly improve others. Even stupid people eventually realize that bad treatment is undeserved. They will eventually respond by withdrawing from you, or by dismissing you entirely. Excessive negativity does not make a person better, again showing how the mean stupid person can generate unintended consequences by taking things to extremes.

Negative emotions can only spur someone to improve when they are sincere and are part of a mix of emotions that together make a mature personality. This mix does not exist for stupid people who are negative too often.

Still, you cannot always convince negative stupid people to act appropriately. An excessive amount of mean treatment can certainly feel bad, but you have the power to shut it down. Fulfill your own needs by simply saying no to those who mistreat you or ask too much from you. If you choose not to do this, but have the power to do so, it becomes your fault, not theirs.

Life is tough, and one of the toughest parts of it is recognizing when you are causing it to be far tougher than it needs to be. Life is even tougher for those who do not have the physical power to protect themselves from negative interactions. This type of situation happens more frequently than you may think, and it causes untold amounts of harm. It puts lesser issues, which are the main focus of this book, into the proper perspective that they can otherwise lack.

The mind is highly malleable, but it does not always change instantly and easily to exactly what you want. Sometimes it changes to protect the rest of your mind. There are limits to what each of us can do, and improvement is the goal even when it is not immediately an option.

Chapter 31: Anxiety, the chapter that you are too scared to read

I have already mentioned that everyone has stress. I expect howling disagreement from many stupid people on this. They will say, "I don't have stress! I'm not weak!" in ways that indicate both stress and weakness. One cannot be defensive without having felt stress in some way. Strong people do not need to desperately deny or hide something to make themselves feel better. Strong people do not have to respond in desperate ways at all in normal conversations.

As usual, stupid people believe that stress must be 100% present or absent from a person, not realizing that real phenomena exist independent from such fanciful extremes. The above mentioned tough stupid people would be better off saying that they do not have crippling anxiety. I do not mean to focus too much on the distinction between stress and anxiety. Goodness knows that stupid people believe that both these words indicate something that is as irreversible as a building falling on your head.

The worst kinds of anxiety can occur in a few ways. Some people cannot help it due to neurochemical imbalances that require medication. Others are very much capable of helping it. Even those who need medication are not instantly cured by it. At some stage, we must all do what we can cognitively to recognize and manage anxiety. Tough people have a valid method for doing so among many possible methods, which involves saying what I put into their mouths above. Even when obviously wrong about what they say, they can still do that part in way that is good enough to get by.

Stupid people are not in the habit of questioning their emotions. After all, if you are feeling blinding rage, sadness, boredom, or disappointment, it is not possible to resist that or feel something else, right? Wrong of course. Stupid people cannot imagine feeling something different from what they are currently feeling, and they cannot imagine that they are mistaken in their current feelings. This can be a relatively minor issue where most emotions are concerned, but it is worse when it comes to anxiety.

There are very few situations where anxiety will help you. If a predator is about to eat you, anxiety helps keep you focused on that immediate problem. If you need to prepare something and are not doing so, then anxiety is the emotional kick in the butt that your mind can deliver to you. Stupid people misunderstand this most of the time, just sitting there dwelling in the anxiety instead of doing whatever they need to do.

In the vast majority of situations, anxiety only makes things worse by distracting you from any useful thoughts. Simply put, most problems can be solved at our leisure and therefore do not require anxiety to continuously kick us in the pants. Sometimes anxiety is pointless because there is no danger. Sometimes it is pointless because it concerns things that did not or will not happen. Sometimes it is felt concerning issues that are purely imaginary. Being evidence-free, problems based on purely fanciful notions are more difficult to resolve than problems that are based on anything real.

Many stupid people become highly anxious whenever they believe that they have done something wrong, even when the wrongness of what they have done is highly subjective or insignificant. This anxiety prevents them from learning from their mistakes.

It is not always easy to pick apart why a mistake has occurred, and if people are so anxiety-stricken that they cannot remember what they did wrong, then they are very likely to repeat mistakes. There is no shame in being wrong. There is shame in doing the exact same wrong things repeatedly over long periods of time.

Memories of traumatic events can continue to circulate inside the mind for years. These memories permeate every perception, being additionally associated with others who never said or did the things that the memories are based upon. This can become all-consuming and all-encompassing, gaining a vastly exaggerated scope. Other books have said this, but it can never be said enough: If you are still bothered by the memory of a mistake that you made 10 years ago, then you are the one maintaining the problem.

Even tough stupid people can go through enough anxiety that they need to vent it, which they often do by redirecting it through projecting, inappropriately making accusations against people who did nothing. Revoke their permission to do this, unless you like being pushed around by those who have only one more clue than you do. If they are tough, they will find a real solution instead of pushing you around.

Chapter 32: The evils of self-evaluation, even self-approval

It is well-known that societies went through a phase where some stupid people tried to convince everyone that we are all very special and precious, and that we are even more special if we feel bad about ourselves or differ from societal concepts of perfection. This was a very misguided and lazy set of ideas that quickly met with opposition from every side, but often for stupid reasons. Specialness became a sort of reverse currency, where people wanted to have preferably zero specialness because specialness was taken to indicate that something irreparable was wrong with them.

Some of the opposition to this terrible phase expressed concerns that a focus on self-praise would result in widespread narcissism. One might even gain the idea from these concerns that narcissism is a bad thing! Outrageous! It is a bad thing, but only because it results in abuse, unfulfilled lives, and rigid, uncreative thinking. Otherwise narcissism is an easy way for lazy people to become successful, as discussed in a previous chapter.

I acknowledge that self-condemnation is not good, but it is not remedied by "liking oneself," or through self-praise. Such attempted remedies are lazy approaches to a problem that is perceived but not understood. Self-condemnation does not arise from insufficient self-praise. It arises from internalizing and reliving condemnation that comes from others.

Praise can be called a possible opposite of condemnation from one perspective, but it does not reverse or nullify the ideas conveyed by condemnation. Praise is also highly vulnerable to being perceived as insincere. There is considerable cultural awareness of bootlickers who praise for dishonest reasons. There is much less awareness of how condemnation can be inaccurate or dishonest. We tend to trust condemnation as having some element of truth, especially when it is delivered as a reaction. We do not often consider how a condemner could be simply mistaken.

Our minds tend to relive feedback and impactful spoken words that we have previously encountered. An internal authority figure is formed through all of this, strongly reflecting one's own personality. It is not good when the internal authority figure is a hater, but it is also not good when it is a shameless flatterer. In other words, any authority figure, internal or external, is much more effective when it delivers plain old truth and honest advice. It becomes strongly dysfunctional when it wanders too far from this in either a positive or negative direction.

As an alternate solution, I suggest getting rid of self-evaluation. Do not tell yourself that you are bad. Do not tell yourself that you are good. I can guarantee that you are neither good nor bad. What you have done and said could have had good or bad results, but they must be examined as independent from the self. As I have said, it does not matter who tells you that 2+2=5, it is still wrong. Following that same reasoning, you can improve your habits and beliefs by not perceiving them as belonging to you.

Chapter 33: The primal elements of stupid behavior

In our thought processes, we stupid people retain a potentially surprising number of conclusions that could be called primal. These conclusions can also be called childish, deeply corrupt, or even apparently evil, conflicting with all lessons that society has intentionally tried to teach us. Many of us have instead learned what society has unintentionally taught us.

The distinction between words and belief may never be greater than in the contrast between what societies say versus what they enforce. This is not because of any sinister mind controlling villain directing any part of society. It is because we are primarily creatures of appetite, capable of occasional rational thoughts, instead of being rational creatures with occasional appetites.

Rational thought is a strange accident of the mind that happens to be favored for the long-term survival of societies. It is not exactly who we are.

Many concepts that are rationally rejected are strongly accepted on a primal level. For instance, the idea of a "bully" is rationally rejected. Yet, individuals love bullies on a primal level. Because of this, it is never really an insult to call someone a bully. You may not situationally like it when bullies attack you, but you do like it when they attack those who you also wish to attack.

When you call someone a bully, you are always complimenting them, because you are calling them strong. This touches upon another highly influential primal concept: the idea of strength versus weakness. Many rejected ideas are wrongly associated with weakness, simply because some apparently weak person tried and failed to support them. I am not talking solely about physical weakness. Cognitive weakness, such as cognitive dissonance, comes into play as well. Even stupid people are very quick to pick up on many kinds of weakness, which they will strongly reject at their convenience. For these reasons, if you want to insult a bully, then focus on something that accompanies failure instead of strength. So-called bullies are often weak or otherwise flawed in many ways, for instance, and if you pay attention you will notice this.

This is not to say that stupid people have any perfect way to recognize weakness. Physical strength is usually easy to distinguish from physical weakness, but emotional strength is much more subtle and stupid people frequently get it backwards. Stupid people frequently mistake desperation for strength, but desperation is actually a sign of weakness. This type of weakness does not guarantee failure, but desperate people are very likely to fail spectacularly because they will not be able to deal with challenges that require lateral thinking regarding anything beyond their own fears.

I suspect that at least some of you are not convinced by what I just said. Think it over. Strong and skilled people do not often need to be desperate. They do not often need to resort to extreme measures to get something done. Weak and unskilled people require posturing and bluffing to attain goals that that they fear to attempt through effort.

Despite anyone's awareness of all this, stupid people will remain mistaken when they misinterpret things primally. This creates issues. At the very least, this requires us to spend extra time planning around the failings of these stupid people.

A stupid fear of weakness increases the cost of nice behavior, since stupid people are prone to mistake nice behavior as a form of repression or primal submission.

Patience becomes feared as a potential form of weakness, because it involves a temporary delay in pursuit of appetites.

Apologies become universally shunned, because they are also seen as forms of submission.

All of this promotes dysfunctional behaviors such as never apologizing for anything, contributing to a societal inability to honestly resolve disagreements and learn from them. It also requires otherwise friendly and rational people to behave in dysfunctional ways when they know better, just to make life easier for stupid people who do things wrongly.

Conclusion: Isn't self-help supposed to make you feel better?

I find it very likely that you may feel a little worse after reading this far, instead of feeling better. It is somewhat well-known that increased awareness does not necessarily lead to increased happiness. Properly used awareness, however, can lead to great happiness, and this is what stupid people do not understand. Some people tell others to get off their lawns. I instead tell stupid people that they are stupid. This section will list some reasons why we do not have nice things, followed by some ways that we can gain them if we find the effort to be worthwhile.

Many stupid people have everything that they need, but they use it all poorly. They overuse or misuse tools available to them. They lazily approach important jobs in ways that reduce any positive effects that they could have on themselves and their loved ones. Stupid people have the potential to use everything they have properly and usefully, if only doing the right thing did not bore them.

We are poorly equipped for helping others. Selfishness is deeply ingrained in us even when we do our best to eliminate it: it sneaks into our minds, expressing itself in creative new ways. We have tendencies to flip to one conceptual extreme or another, without ever visiting anything in between, which causes idealistic helpers to become cynics over time.

Problems arise when people decide that behavior does not matter, yet it matters intensely. Every major problem results from the immediate or extenuating circumstances of many petty weaknesses such as laziness, envy, stupidity, and other well-known failures of human nature. Greater problems result from accepting these weaknesses as the undeniable way of things.

It is fair to ask if I have said anything positive in this whole book. I have, but you may not remember it. A day or so after reading this book, you will probably gain the impression that I said essentially, "People are stupid, and they are stupid, and they are double-dog stupidy-stupid." This is what happens when people read books and try to remember them later. They boil it all down to a grossly oversimplified one-liner, which would save considerable time and money if only books were actually that short. This is not that kind of book.

I advise reading this book again, then reading it backwards, and then reading it under purple light. Well, maybe not that last part. Eventually you will find something positive, but some of the book does tell you to put a limit on what positive things are said. Being blindly positive does not help much. Informed positive statements are far better, gained when you know how to believably reject excessive negativity.

I will be honest here by saying that stupidity can take an effectively infinite number of forms. I do not know your particular brand of stupidity. I hope that you find part of yourself in this book, but it is possible that you will not. There is no way to find and specifically provide solutions for every brand of stupidity, but I can tell you some simple solutions to frequent causes of the misery caused by stupidity. Much of this is so simple that you may never believe it works, but it does. Think of it this way: after you have had exactly the same thought millions of times over more than ten years, everything else probably seems deceptively simple in comparison.

At some stage in life, the immature, broken, coddled, or abusive motivating thoughts in a person's mind need to be recognized and culled, in order for a stupid person to become smart. This requires being able to tell the difference between an unhelpful thought versus a helpful one, which is a very tall task for stupid people. It requires them to separate their concepts of themselves from the things that they think and do, which is again not expected. "Put this off until later" needs to be replaced with, "If not now, then when?" for instance. Replace "I deserve to be yelled at," with "I am just as good as this person, and do not deserve abuse from them." The mistaken belief that you cannot do anything important in life can be replaced by an awareness of important things that you could do. Be willing to laugh at yourself, because people who cannot laugh at themselves are never earnestly laughing at all. I could go on, but hopefully you get the picture. This process can be called becoming a mature person.

It is not as easy as it sounds to become mature, because today's stupid teacher is our entertainment, and mature entertainment is tough to find. For someone who has rarely or never noticed a mature voice giving good advice, becoming smart may well be impossible. More positive and effective role models could help alleviate all of this, but who does that?

The difficulty in providing succinct good advice on this is that there are so many ways of being stupid. There are stupid people who are too mean to themselves but too nice to others, some who are too mean to themselves and others, those who are nice to everyone but too self-indulgent, and the list goes on to effectively infinite lengths. If we found out a way to stamp out all known forms of stupidity, more would be invented. However, a stupid mind is capable of undoing what it does. If the mind makes near-infinite stupidity, then the mind can just as well undo all that stupidity.

Many stupid people have a mischievous need to remain stupid, even when you point out problems and appropriately provide easy ways to remedy the situation. This reveals that stupidity is often a comfort zone that has been chosen and internalized.

It is very difficult to convince a comfortably stupid person to change, because the perception of necessity is not there. They can become drunk off the surplus of attention that they receive when someone tries to change them, and this will instead often change them only in ways that you did not want.

After all, if a person is feeling drunk off attention, they are very likely to change in ways that yield more of that intoxicating attention. This is why you are best advised to let stupid people change themselves instead of trying to directly change them.

If you want to change a stupid person, then create a necessity. Fit into their broken world view, instead of simply telling them that a functional world exists outside of it (they will not believe this).

I discussed a cause for hope in an earlier chapter, under the name of mood health. This is one of the few things that can consistently spur you to do good. Most incentives in human lives function through simple survival, reproduction, and social acceptance, therefore being morally neutral, but mood health is something at least slightly different from that. Doing good things and knowing it, while not getting an undeserved reward, grants increased mood health and can help improve you and your surroundings.

The opposite effect stems from poor mood health: excessive guilt, desire for revenge, envy, hatred, for instance. All of these emotions feel bad, but we may dwell in them anyway through habit and because we are aware of perceived needs that have not been met. Many times we can meet these needs through living more functionally, but we may ignore this option because of the narrow mindset that accompanies intense emotions.

Why then, are actions that promote good mood health relatively rare? They feel good, and are good for everyone. However, increased mood health does not necessarily increase your chances of addressing the other incentives in your life. Charity, for instance, is available mainly for those who are already comfortable in life in some way. It is less available for those who are struggling in many ways.

The remainder of this section will be devoted to those who were born into struggles. I plan to show that you have some advantages as well, if not as many as those who are born into comfort.

You are, in part, what you think. If you have many cynical thoughts, you will ooze cynicism. If you have many cheerful thoughts, you will be mainly cheerful. If you believe that others have cheated you, will be mainly unfulfilled. It does not matter if you have these thoughts about yourself or others. It does not matter if they are true or false.

Your mind distinguishes things poorly on underlying levels. When you experience strong emotions, you will associate them with what inspired you to feel that way, but you will also associate them with surrounding objects that had no part in generating them. Likewise, if you think something about another person, there will be some reflection of the same thought onto yourself. You may ask if you should just think good thoughts then, and everything is fine, right? Wrong, at least partly.

Good thoughts have a purpose, but they usually do not fix everything all by themselves. Good thoughts do not fix injustice. If you do not have food or clean water, good thoughts alone will not generate them for you. Good thoughts alone will not stop a person who is determined to take what you own.

Stupid people are simple individuals with simple problems. They think a great deal, inefficiently, about those problems without solving anything, thereby blowing their problems outrageously far out of proportion. The solutions to most stupid person problems are so simple that it can seem silly to even discuss them. This is not helped when the entire concept of solving a problem is alien to some stupid people. Others dodge solutions because they fear being bored without fabricated problems.

Most stupid people dismiss and forget simple things that can make their lives better, trudging through life with the same simple problems that they do not address.

Make a list of what you need every day. Look at it and ask yourself if you can get these things. If you cannot, then write down exactly what is stopping you. Vague reasons will not do. What exactly is stopping you? Eventually, you will arrive at a root issue that can be addressed. This will not instantly solve all problems, but it will help. Always try to improve yourself and your situation in life. Small steps are fine, and may even be best for this. Instead of focusing on how you feel, which is generally useless, focus upon what you can do about it. Always give yourself power, instead of taking it away.

While we are on this subject, I will tell you that I do not want to hear about your pain. Everyone has pain. I want to hear about your strength. Strength is shown by what you do despite your pain, and not everyone shows it. You may dismiss strength because every fictional protagonist has it. In real life, failure is everywhere, and it is not so interesting. There are many ways to fail, and many of them are easy paths to follow. Real people with real strength are fascinating because they are comparatively rare.

View everything as an opportunity. For instance, if you make a mistake, it is an opportunity to learn. This leads to creative thinking that can put petty issues out of the way. I am not going to say that guilt over mistakes will instantly disappear, but it will probably not last in your mind unresolved for 50 years.

Do not dwell on self-labels. If you refuse to follow this advice, then why not go whole-hog and buy a labeling gun? Label yourself with the words that you have wrongly attached to yourself in your mind. This is better than keeping it inside and never properly thinking about it.

Live with enthusiasm. If you cannot do so right now, then go back to the paragraph about lists and follow it until you can. Do not go through life in a passive daze, stagnating in fear, worry, or despondency, never making any progress. Life is not lived well by capable people who choose helplessness. Tackle all challenges with enthusiasm. If you find yourself dreading anything, find a way to stamp out that dread. No matter what you are facing, the human mind is flexible enough to do this. After all, we live in a world with more scientific knowledge than ever, yet people will tell you about Bigfoot and the Flat Earth all day long if you cannot find a way to escape. With all that going on, I will not let you tell me that your mind cannot convince itself of something.

Never wallow in worry. Excessive worrying is what helpless people do. It can be an emotional kick in the pants to get lazy people off the couch, but its purpose ends there. Wallowing in worry indicates that you will never leave the couch. Some stupid people shape their entire lives around paralyzing worry, which is a pitiful waste that is far worse than whatever they are worrying about. Let me tell you this: worrying does not prevent bad things from happening. Excessive worrying causes problems. Functional people anticipate and prepare. Stupid people worry and never do anything about it.

Lift the limits on currencies such as attention and acceptance. Learn to work with people who differ in appearance, mannerisms, or opinions. Learn how to help others who will benefit and reciprocate, instead of those why are simply crying louder. We live in a culture where billionaires are given more money because they whine louder. They show that whiners are winners when everyone is stupid. Do I need to tell you how bad that is?

Admit it when you make a mistake, and then take steps to learn from it. Let others be right when they are right, even if you do not like it. Give others permission to show inner strength. Forgive the small stuff and use it for teaching, but punish the big stuff.

Making things better is a burden that everyone shoulders every day. It is not simply the responsibility of that one person that you do not like. It is not evaded or remedied by the people that you like. You do not escape this through doing only one thing right on one day. Extreme awareness of all this will not make you immune. Those who fail at bearing this burden are not always the worst people.

In order to be better, you must want to be better, enjoying the process of becoming better or understanding that the benefits are worth it. If you enjoy living the life that you have made for yourself, your personality will be energetic, and everyone will notice this. This will teach through example, which is one of the best ways of teaching. Hating those who do not do some or any of this, is to be stupid.

Inspirations for this book

You may want to avoid any book that is remotely similar to this one, which is fair enough. If you instead want more giant kicks in the behind, I wonder what you are into, but some of these publications will be more than happy to oblige. Others are worth reading because they could open your mind just a slight bit. This book would be much worse without the inspiration provided by these sources.

The Subtle Art of Not Giving a Fuck. Mark Manson. This is the most proximal influence on my Stupid Book. It opened my eyes to the idea that an author can add a resilient and helpful guiding voice to your life. It speaks in ways that make sense even to stupid people. Also check out his newer book, Everything is Fucked, a Book About Hope. I have not yet found time to read it because I write stupid books, but I am sure that it is not terrible.

No More Mr. Nice Guy. Robert A. Glover. Another very strong influence, it explains how many of us are way too nice for our own good, which does not have nice results for us and our loved ones. While primarily for men, it is great for women as well because they are not immune to these same stupid behaviors.

Emotional Intelligence 2.0. Travis Bradberry & Jean Greaves. Most of us need to gain some emotional intelligence. This is not the only book on the subject out there, but it is among the ones that you are most likely to find as a stupid person. I sincerely hope that you will learn from this that you are not the only conscious person in the world. However, since you are nothing but a baby who accidentally grew taller and went through puberty, I doubt this will actually happen.

I hesitate to cite some of the older classics because stupid people will misunderstand them all and break something. Most likely however, you will only get bored and drift away to arguing on the Internet instead, rendering all these recommendations harmless in comparison to the damage that you are already doing to your mind.

If you are an educated stupid person, Philosophical Dictionary by Voltaire is a good fun read and not really a dictionary. If you are a scientific/philosophical stupid person, Karl Popper's books are useful but not exactly page turners. You almost certainly will not have time to read them. For humor, special mention goes to Will Cuppy.

Religious stupid people will go to some bad place comparable to Hades no matter what they do, but if you are religious, you should at least try to read the actual material that your religion is based on. I was just joking when I said that it was bad to do so. You get jokes, right?

I pity you political stupid people, but you should try to read something, anything, that is not about politics. You could read political crap for a thousand years and not learn one damned thing.